missionsmart
15 critical questions to ask
before launching overseas

David L. Frazier

"Without counsel plans fail,
but with many advisers they succeed."
Proverbs 15:22

Written and published as a ministry of
Equipping Servants International (ESI)
P.O. Box 770835
Memphis, Tennessee 38117 USA
www.esionline.org

"...for the equipping of the saints for the work of service."
  Ephesians 4:12

First Edition 2014
www.createspace.com

Cover Photo - www.shutterstock.com
Chapter photos used in accordance with the license
agreements of the following websites:
www.creativecommons.com
www.sxc.hu websites

ISBN-13: 978-1492339267
ISBN-10: 1492339261

Dedicated to my wife Vicki
and my daughters Elizabeth and Emily
who have always believed in me

Acknowledgments

Sir Isaac Newton said, "*If I have seen a little further, it is by standing on the shoulders of giants.*" As I look back, I am grateful to all the friends, mentors, teachers and colleagues that have shown me my faults, shared their wisdom, and patiently taught me through the years. This book compiles my own mistakes, observations, readings, courses, and lessons from others. I write it with a heart of gratitude to God and His people, with a passion for His glory among the nations, and with a joy to be in His service among such wonderful friends.

I thank my Heavenly Father who sent His Son Jesus as a missionary to earth to seek and save a wretch like me. I am grateful to my earthly father, Thomas W. Frazier, Sr., for teaching me to work hard, be responsible, walk humbly, and laugh a lot. My dear mother, Mary Ann Frazier, taught me to pray without ceasing, to trust in God's good and sovereign hand in everything, to walk in the joy of the Lord every day, and to pour my life into others. I have appreciated my brothers Tom, Tim, Dan, and Jon for encouraging me along the way and passing on wisdom for life. I also thank God for giving me such wonderful in-laws, Charles and Jean Coleman, who have given so much support and have been there for us through thick and thin.

Thank you, Heno Head, for my wonderful camp experiences and for exhibiting Jesus Christ to me more than any other ever has. My church youth leaders, Bill Neal and David Morris, showed me how to live with convictions and share my life with others. My mentor Michael Kerns has taught me how to discern my calling, serve in my giftings, and walk before an audience of One. I thank God for my other friends and colleagues in the U.S. and abroad who have given me encouragement to press on and be faithful to my calling.

Vicki, my life partner in this journey, has taught me how to love with compassion, listen with the heart, and be patient with God's work in others. We have seen the world together, lived among and embraced a people group, raised two amazing girls overseas. I look forward to more adventures! Much of who I am and what I have learned comes from my dear wife.

Charlemagne said, "*To have another language is to possess a second soul.*" With this second soul, I have had the joy of deep friendships that have given me unique perspectives on God, life, and culture. Thank you, Duzgun, Halil, and Ferudun, for letting me into your lives and teaching me so much. May God finally pour out His Spirit upon your people and bring a great harvest of worshipers to the throne of the Lamb!

Few have the privilege of being a part of the same local church their entire lives. I will be forever grateful to the people of First Evangelical Church in Memphis, TN, for the love, support, prayers, and encouragement they have given to me since I was born.

I thank Columbia International University for granting me a scholarship to research and study the material in this book and for providing such knowledgeable and godly teachers to refresh and guide me in my journey.

Tom Frazier, Robert Cline, Seth Stevens and Don Gilbert have given invaluable input regarding content. I greatly appreciate Stacy Tyson for his help in bringing this book to print. Finally, I am indebted to Chuck and Carolyn Downs for their friendship and support since the earliest days of our missional journey and for their labor of love in editing the manuscript.

DLF 2014

About the Author

David has been involved in cross-cultural ministry and equipping believers for over twenty-five years. He completed his undergraduate degree in Inter-cultural Studies and World Missions at Biola University and later earned an M.A. degree in General Theological Studies from Columbia International University. Before moving to the Middle East, he and his wife, Vicki, ministered to internationals in their hometown of Memphis, Tennessee, USA. David also has an M.A. in English with a concentration in Teaching English as a Second Language, which has enabled him to build relationships with internationals and obtain a legitimate platform overseas. He uses his twenty years of overseas work, mentorship, teaching, and cross-cultural living to equip and train others to reach the unreached. His passion is to mentor young singles and couples in finding their callings and becoming equipped to fulfill them.

David and Vicki lead *Equipping Servants International,* a ministry that mentors individuals, trains churches and advises mission agencies. Their desire is to equip God's people to do healthier candidate assessment, pre-field training, and on-field guidance for cross-cultural ministers both at home and abroad. They also help other ministries become wiser stewards of their funds and people in missional endeavors.

For more information and to arrange for training or consulting, please refer to their website: **www.esionline.org**

Table of Contents

Preface

〜 Josh and Sara sat nervously waiting for the church missions pastor to come into the room. The couple had chosen a people group and found a mission agency that wanted them, but they needed their home church approval. Their passports had just arrived in the mail, and they were excited about this new adventure in their lives. When the pastor came in, he picked up a clip-board from his desk and sat down across from them. He smiled and said, "So you want to be missionaries?" He began to ask them questions about calling, giftedness, and confirmation. He then asked about their past experience, present ministry, and lifestyle. As questions were asked, the couple would often look at each other with confused glances and sometimes were unable to answer. Until this day, no one had been asking these kinds of questions. This line of questioning had revealed some holes in their understanding and plans. Josh and Sara suddenly realized they needed to take more steps to confirm their calling, test their giftings, and better equip themselves for this vocation. The

So You Want to be a Missionary?

pastor stopped in the middle of his list and put the clipboard down. Instead of giving approval to the couple, he suggested they lay out a plan of action for the coming year.

The theme of God seeking *"to proclaim [His] name through all the earth"* and gather worshipers to His throne pervades Scripture (Exodus 9:16). We see **a missionary God** who is on a mission to all the peoples of the world. His Church in the world is His vehicle to fulfill His mission. We are all called to be about God's mission to the world. It is encouraging, therefore, to see many today desiring to go out to the nations to live out and share the message of Jesus Christ with the unreached peoples of the world. These Christians desire to live among a people group and engage in cross-cultural ministry.

Statistics tell us that many people—particularly Americans—who board a plane and head overseas for long-term, cross-cultural ministry end up struggling on the field. Often they return home after a few years quite beat up spiritually and emotionally. They fail to learn the language well. They fail to acculturate to the new environment. They fail to connect with and impact the target people. Others have such bitter conflicts with fellow Christian workers that they leave the field in discouragement and disillusionment. The result? Mission failure, broken dreams, and great loss of resources. Who suffers? The name of Christ, the family themselves, the target people group, and the local sending church. In addition, a huge loss of financial resources results. We must ask some critical questions: Why is this happening? How can we do better? What distinguishes those who not only survive but also thrive overseas and achieve effective service?

Before skipping to any other part of this book, please read the **Introduction - Filling the Gaps**. This section will help you better understand what is missing in the entire missions mobilization process, from "feeling a call" to actually landing overseas. One purpose of this book is to fill these gaps in the journey. The following chapters will deal with some practical but essential issues a person must work through before even considering long-term cross-cultural ministry overseas.

This book is not designed to be a missionary training program. Providing what you need for learning a language, engaging in cross-cultural evangelism, and establishing healthy indigenous churches are indeed important subjects. Let's first, however, address the steps one should take and the questions one should ask when considering cross-cultural ministry overseas. Crossing an ocean does not make one a missionary. We want those pursuing cross-cultural work to gain a better understanding of themselves, their callings, and the necessary preparation. Let all who enter overseas ministry do it with their eyes wide open! We hope to foster right thinking about overseas endeavors and to encourage a healthy understanding of the task. Avoid mission failures and fatigue. Know your calling and how to fulfill it successfully.

⁓ *The missions pastor told Josh and Sara that he was not trying to discourage them from engaging in global outreach or to cause them to abandon their vision. He said he simply wanted to guide them and offer a healthier way to proceed in this journey in discovering their place in God's mission to the nations. He wanted to ask the critical questions before they boarded an airplane.*

Using This Book

This book may be used by individuals or small groups. At the end of each chapter, we have added discussion questions as well as homework assignments. While individuals can simply read through the chapters and glean insights for their own mission journey, only half the benefit of this book would be gained. Our desire is that candidates do more than just read about these principles. For the healthiest process in discovering God's calling on someone's life, he or she should plan to work through the questions and homework with a mentor, i.e., someone who has experience in life, ministry, and overseas living. We also hope church leaders and mission mobilizers can incorporate this book into their missionary screening and training programs.

> *For the healthiest process, work through questions and homework with a mentor.*

Discovering God's Will

God typically uses four sources for guiding His children in life decisions: Scripture, Prayer, Providence, and Counsel. We challenge candidates to embrace all of these in their decision-making process. They should have a healthy input of God's Word. They should seek the Lord often in prayer, asking Him to guide them in their journey. God also providentially uses circumstances in life to direct His children. This book falls into the category of Counsel, as it seeks to bring experience to the table and ask questions that can give a new perspective. While recognizing that a person's calling into overseas ministry involves a deep spiritual dynamic, it is our purpose in this book to challenge individuals, churches, and organizations to consider the personal, relational, and practical realities of this vocation.

A Word of Caution

While this book is written as a "checklist" of questions, this list should not be seen as a set of stringent rules to hinder candidates in their equipping process. These questions are meant to be general guiding principles, not a legalistic yoke to force upon candidates. Instead, these guidelines are intended to help people navigate their journey and to understand their particular callings within God's mission to the world. These principles can offer new perspectives upon calling, giftings and cross-cultural ministry as well as assist mission mobilizers as they screen, mentor, and train followers of Christ to know and fulfill their callings in life. When we know our particular callings, we are in a healthy place where God can use us to make our contribution to His mission to the nations, both here and abroad!

These questions are not meant to be a yoke to force upon candidates.

Extra Reading

As part of the Homework Assignments, we recommend candidates read several books listed at the end of each section of the book and record key lessons gained. In addition to these, they can check our website for further suggested readings and resources: www.esionline.org. We also advise the reader to subscribe to *Evangelical Missionary Quarterly* online (www.emisdirect.com). The cost for one year is minimal and gives you access to a rich archive of articles.

Introduction - Filling the Gaps

~ *Family and friends crowded the airport gate to say goodbye to their loved ones. Mark and Amy and their two children were moving overseas to serve the Lord in a far-away land. Everyone waved goodbye as the family boarded the plane. Tears of joy were flowing and hearts were full of inspiration and prayers. No one there could have imagined that after just two years, this same family would be moving back home. This time only a few family members were at the airport. This time their tears flowed from sorrow, and their prayers were asking God to keep the family and their faith intact. So many dreams and hopes had been dashed. They weren't thinking about taking the gospel to the unreached; they were wondering how things could have gone so wrong and trying to figure out how they were going to work through it all.*

The National Aeronautics and Space Administration (NASA) spends an enormous amount of resources and time to research past mission failures.[1] They gather detailed feedback from every sector of the space program and produce thorough reports. Their goal is to discover how they can be more successful in accomplishing their missions with less loss of life and resources.

When Christians who have left their home countries for long-term ministry overseas leave the field early for unexpected reasons, it is called *missionary attrition*. In 1997, the World Evangelical Alliance Missions Commission launched the landmark research project, known as ReMAP (Reducing Missionary Attrition Project), across fourteen countries with 453 sending agencies, to learn about the causes of missionary attrition. From these findings, William D. Taylor prepared the book, *Too Valuable to Lose: Exploring the Causes and Cures of Missionary Attrition*. ReMAP sought to discover the reasons missionaries leave the field and made the following conclusion: *the top issues in preventable attrition had to do with character and relationships*.[2]

Depending on how we define the Protestant and full-time missionary, we can estimate the long-term overseas missionary force at 150,000-300,000.[3] Some difficult fields are seeing more than half of their Christian workers leave within the first five years. The number of missionaries leaving prematurely has increased over the past 20 years.[4] The one-time costs for missionary training and relocation may be $50,000, and the yearly support package around $60,000, so that when a family leaves the field prematurely after three years, the total investment to that point could be as high as $250,000. These figures do not reflect the emotional, personal, and spiritual losses to the family, the church, and the field.

> *...when a family leaves the field pre-maturely after three years, the total investment to that point could be as high as $250,000.*

In light of what has been learned about attrition, it would be beneficial to know the main causes for attrition, but more importantly, what enables some people to achieve long-term, effective cross-cultural ministries. Taylor ends his work with a challenge to identify factors that encourage effective, long-term service.[5] The following chapters present the qualities and skills that can be developed, tested, and proven in potential candidates *pre-field* to enable them to thrive and be effective overseas.

The attrition study shows that while some attrition is unpreventable, for reasons such as health, children's education, retirement, lack of support, aging parents, and political crisis, much attrition is actually preventable. If the main causes for early departure and failure on the field are not oppressive false religions, restrictive governments, inhospitable neighbors, or poor living conditions, then what are they? In fact, the main sources involve areas such as misunderstanding of calling, personal character issues, incorrect fit in ministry giftings, poor relational skills, and insufficient language progress.

Gaps in the Mobilization Process

Where are the gaps in the preparation process and who is responsible for these gaps? Mission agencies? Theological institutions? Pre-field mission training centers? Overseas field and team leadership? Agency member-care? Or does the problem lie with local sending churches? Let's look at each of these.

Foreign Mission Agencies often put too much weight on a local church's stamp of approval of a candidate. Vice versa, churches can put a lot of weight on agency approval. Agency recruiters can be driven by the great needs around the world or by visionary leaders who have set goals to send as many workers to the field as possible. Agencies also have to trust the candidate's calling testimony, letters of reference, and a church's endorsement. Even sending a candidate through a week-long screening process, followed by a pre-field training program, may not be enough to assess a person's calling or giftedness.

Formal and non-formal **Pre-field Mission Training** and **Theological Institutions** are designed mainly to impart knowledge and principles about theology, language acquisition, culture, evangelism, and church planting. Theological institutions do not always have the time or personnel to work through a person's discovery of calling and giftings. Moreover, pre-field training is usually done just before departing to the field. At that point, it is too late to be considering the foundational issues of personal calling, Christian character, relational skills, and cross-cultural giftings.

Overseas Field and Team Leaders are there to enable and coach candidates in the task of fulfilling their callings on a particular field. Overseas leadership may assume all the foundational work has already been done. If it hasn't, those on the field are left to deal with these issues and struggle to attempt to fill in the gaps. If candidates lack the maturity, the gifts or the skills for the job, they will hinder and frustrate a team on the field, create extra work for field leaders, and ultimately waste resources. Agencies and institutions do not and cannot fully develop or evaluate these foundational qualities. If they have not been established prior to leaving, the responsibility falls to the field leaders, teammates, and **Mission Agency Member-Care** staff to handle these basic issues. Ministry focus must then shift to helping these teammates cope and survive, rather than ministering to the locals.

Agencies and institutions do not and cannot fully develop or evaluate these foundational qualities.

Ultimately, the **Candidates** themselves are responsible for discovering if they are called, gifted, and equipped to serve overseas. In the chain of the developmental process, the burden of responsibility next falls on the **Sending Church** and Christian community, who are the ones giving candidates approval and support. If cross-cultural workers need certain qualities to be effective and resilient, once again, the heavy responsibility for development and selection falls on candidates and their home sending churches, not on agencies or training centers.

A home church's stamp of approval lights the fuse and starts a chain reaction which launches the candidate into the process. Likewise, a mission agency's stamp of approval can also launch candidates into the process, when in fact, the candidates may not have had the time or guidance to determine if this is truly their calling. When problems arise, it usually happens later on the field when the pressures of ministry and adaptability reveal stress fractures that could have been detected much earlier.

Churches are giving organizations responsibilities they were never designed or equipped to handle.

Local churches and candidates must take a serious look at the present statistics of missionary attrition and be careful not to assume that agencies or training courses can do all that is needed to screen, counsel, and test candidates. By saying, "*We are not mission agencies,*" churches are giving organizations responsibilities they were never designed or equipped to handle. Local churches can base their decisions for candidate approval upon a powerful testimony, personal contacts in that church, the needy region of the world, or an agency's reputation. But such a basis for decision-making puts the burden for testing and filtering the candidate upon the agency. Later when things on the field go wrong, the church might place the blame upon the agency, the team leadership or the difficulty of the field. Costly member care centers are left to pick up the pieces. This kind of planning is *reactive* instead of *proac-*

tive. When the battered and bruised missionary comes home, the final place of landing is usually the sending church. Here they try to rebuild their lives and find answers to what went so wrong. Often the sending church becomes their recovery center, so why not let it be their discovery center to ensure they are indeed right for the work they are pursuing?

Perhaps the missions enterprise tends to over-emphasize formal theological education, pre-field language/culture training, and church planting methodologies. Maybe we forget that people should find ways to test their calling right here at home, gaining an experiential understanding of the character and giftedness needed to be effective in cross-cultural ministry. Should someone board an airplane to

...not everyone is suited or gifted for ministry in a cross-cultural environment using a foreign language.

go overseas to perform a task they may have never been called to or gifted for and know very little about? Would it not be better if people could *know* their giftings and *test* their callings *before* they left for the field by getting some cross-cultural experience for one or two years here at home and overseas? Would this not give them a clearer understanding as to what is involved as well as show them if they have the abilities and giftedness for this kind of work?

Sending the Wrong People

The missions conference speaker says, "*Stand up if you are ready to go and reach the nations!*" But is everyone who stands supposed to move overseas? Many seem to believe that anyone who desires to serve overseas can go and has the right to be supported in his/her endeavor, especially if the particular field destination is among the most unreached and needy peoples of the world. While every believer in the church today should have a general understanding of other cultures and acquire basic cross-cultural skills in this ever changing multi-ethnic world, not everyone is suited or gifted for long term ministry in a cross-cultural environment using a foreign language. While linguists tell us anyone can learn a foreign language, the fact is not everyone can become fluent enough to evangelize, teach or disciple in a cross-cultural context. For example, someone could be more useful in an English-speaking ministry overseas. Let's guide each candidate to the right ministry for his/her strengths and abilities.

Perhaps the high attrition we are seeing today stems from our sending the wrong people into the wrong kinds of work for them. Nothing is more miserable than to be in a job for which we are not gifted or effective! No matter how needy the field or how "super-spiritual" overseas work may appear, people need to know who God has made *them* to be and what He has called them to do in His mission to the nations. Some are to go, but many are to stay here and work with the internationals living among us. Some are to focus on discipleship, some on giving, and some on prayer. But all of us are to make our contribution in God's mission to gather the peoples of the world to Himself.

Generational Differences

Missiological research has revealed other important findings on missionary attrition (*see Chart 1 on next page*).[6] These studies show a generational gap. As the years have passed, attitudes and perspectives have changed significantly on issues such as length of commitment, career changes, family roles, and authority among the different generations of mission mobilizers and missionaries. Although the 1997 chart reflecting the different generational perspectives of boosters, boomers, and busters is somewhat outdated, churches and agencies have testified to even more shifts in the same direction among millennials (born 1984-2000's). Millennials value

Chart 1: A Generational Perspective on Missions Issues

Issue	Boosters (1927-1945)	Boomers (1946-1964)	Busters (1965-1983)
Call	Mystical	Best job fit	"Best" mission often most caring
Focus of commitment	Particular people or country w/ particular mission organization	Ministry in which and wherever gifts are best used	Particular project
Length of commitment	Life	Short term and review	Short term
Attitude to mission agency	High loyalty	Low loyalty	Low loyalty
Leadership	Authoritarian, respect status	Participatory, consensus, respect competence	Participatory team, respect genuineness and openness
Approach to conflict	Indirect or denial	Clarify and work toward reconciliation	Direct, open, and honest
Attitude to support and pastoral care	Independent	Expect opportunity for both, willing to try and see	Perceive both as essential to well-being
Role issues	Generalists, prepared to do anything, make do	Specialists, pursue excellence, agents of change	Function best in teams, each with focused ministry
Wives' roles	Supporting husband	Contribution in own right	Prefer husband-wife team, egalitarian marriage
Devotional life	No Bible, no breakfast	Wherever it can be fitted in	Find discipline hard but long for spiritual things
Relationship to local community	Paternalistic	Fraternalistic	Work well under church

personal freedoms, privacy, and technology. They strive to provide equal opportunities for all, to protect the environment, and to eliminate injustices.[7]

Previous generations of missionaries can teach us much about commitment and perseverance. While these older generations may expect the same approach to missions from today's generation and preach it at conferences, much of the attrition we see today may be caused by an old mission system trying to challenge, guide, and equip a new generation of missionaries and keep them on the field. The old system does not want to "compromise" the way they have been doing missions, and the new generation of candidates does not want to "compromise" their values about calling, organization, roles, and leadership.

> *...we need a new way of screening, counseling, and equipping this present generation of cross-cultural workers.*

Instead of trying to force these two together, we need a new way of screening, counseling, and equipping this present generation of cross-cultural workers. A new approach does not need to compromise biblical standards of commitment, character, servanthood, and family. But instead of beating young people over the head with "*Young people today are just wimps; in the old days...*" we are proposing a new way of dealing with a new generation. All of us want the same results: committed, humble, cross-cultural servants who can achieve long-term effective service. We simply need a different way of mobilizing God's people today.

To summarize, no theological school, cross-cultural training institute, expert agency screening system, ideal team environment, or well-staffed member-care group can make someone thrive and be effective overseas if their character, giftings, and skills have not already been developed, tested and proven over time in a home church and local international community. Taylor says,

> *When the complex factors of attrition are reduced to their simplest components, the evidence undergirds the importance of a careful selection process guided by standards that are bound neither by culture nor by time.*[8]

Instead of pining for the old days,

> *prospective missionaries need to be more adequately briefed and counseled on the type of spiritual dynamics that will be necessary for survival and successful ministry on the field.*[9]

Filling the Gaps

When sending churches become more proactive in the assessment and guidance process, and when cross-cultural ministry candidates become more proactive in their own personal missions discovery journeys, we will see less attrition, a better use of our resources, and more effective and thriving cross-cultural workers.

Our purpose in this book is not to discourage mission endeavors or dishearten candidates from entering this fulfilling vocation. We simply want those considering overseas cross-cultural living and ministry to know themselves, be sure of their callings and understand the task before them. With the help of this book, discussion questions, and homework assignments, we hope to see people sent out as healthier, better prepared and properly equipped cross-cultural servants. Let's fill these gaps between the local church and the mission agency, between the "calling" and the "going," between the missions conference and the airport!

⟿   Mark and Amy found some temporary housing to have time to work through this transition back to the States. During counseling sessions with pastors and former missionaries, they realized they had not fully understood their callings, their giftings, and the task before them. They had not taken the time to test their calling to cross-cultural ministry prior to moving overseas. Mark had not given Amy a chance to experience cross-cultural hospitality and living. Their pre-field lifestyle had not reflected the one to which they believed they were called. They see now how they had not begun to live out their callings and prepare themselves for this vocation before heading overseas. In hindsight, they wish they had been more teachable, had sought out more advice, and had submitted to the guidance of others prior to pursuing this vocation. Instead of focusing on their failures, Mark and Amy planned to continue with counseling and work on discovering their true callings and giftings in life.

Discussion Questions (Group or Mentor)

1. What missionary attrition have you seen among friends or churches?

2. From what you have learned, what do you see are the main causes?

3. What are the gaps you see in the missionary candidate process?

4. What do you think of a speaker challenging everyone and anyone to consider overseas cross-cultural ministry?

5. Do you think anyone can be trained and effective in this kind of work?

6. Explain your own understanding of a "call to overseas ministry."

7. Who has the main responsibility to screen a candidate properly?

8. What would be some good ways to see a calling tested, ministry gifts confirmed, and skills developed prior to heading overseas?

Homework Assignments

1. Research the missionary attrition at your church. You do not need to include names, etc., just basic statistics. (1 pg)

2. Interview two or three people who have several years of overseas ministry experience and ask them the following: (1-2 pg)

> Their thoughts on the main causes of missionary attrition on the field

> Their advice on how to prepare to avoid premature exit from field

> Ways in which their callings and giftings were confirmed pre-field

Introduction Notes

1 *Report of the Presidential Commission on the Space Shuttle Challenger Accident* (Washington, D.C.: U.S. Government Printing Office, 1986), 1.

2 William David Taylor and World Evangelical Fellowship, *Too Valuable to Lose: Exploring the Causes and Cures of Missionary Attrition* (Pasadena: William Carey Library, 1997), 13.

3 Ibid., 13.

4 Jim Van Meter, "U.S. Report of Findings on Missionary Retention," December 2003. http://www.worldevangelicals. org/resources/view.htm?id=95 (Accessed August 6, 2013)

5 Taylor and World Evangelical Fellowship, *Too Valuable to Lose*, 357.

6 Kath Donovan and Ruth Myors, "Reflections on Attrition in Career Missionaries: A Generational Perspective into the Future," in *Too Valuable to Lose: Exploring the Causes and Cures of Missionary Attrition, William David Taylor and World Evangelical Fellowship*, (Pasadena: William Carey Library, 1997), 48.

7 "Connected, Yet Divided: Telefónica Survey of the Millennial Generation Reveals Digital Natives Are Optimistic About Their Individual Futures." http://blog.digital.telefonica. com/?press-release=telefonica-millennial-survey-findings (Accessed August 5, 2013)

8 Taylor and World Evangelical Fellowship, *Too Valuable to Lose*, 205.

9 Deseree Whittle, "Missionary Attrition: Its Relationship to the Spiritual Dynamics of the Late Twentieth Century," *Caribbean Journal of Evangelical Theology* 3 (1999), 79.

Part I

The PERSON

If we desire to become an astronaut,
before we ever see a rocket, before we can even enter
the NASA training program, we must first go through
a candidate screening process to see if we even have
the basic qualifications and fitness.

Likewise, if someone desires to become a overseas,
cross-cultural missionary, this PERSON must go
through a screening process
and ask some critical questions.

Chapter 1

Checking Heart Motivations

Why Are You Going?

"Take care lest your heart be deceived, and you turn aside and serve other gods and worship them."
Deuteronomy 11:16

~~ It had been several years since Alan and Wendy had arrived in the Middle East. They had taken good steps towards learning the culture and language. They were trying to embrace a simpler lifestyle and acculturate to the local customs. They were building some relationships with locals in the community. The couple was serving in a local indigenous church, hoping to come alongside believers to encourage and empower them. Everything seemed to be going according to the ideal they had set for themselves. But over the course of six months, each of their *relationships and ministry plans began to unravel until they were left with nothing. They became discouraged and felt their work had all been for naught. Their discouragement turned to depression, and plans were made to return to their home country. Alan and Wendy were confused by how this spiritual depression had come upon them. They felt so ineffective and hopeless. What had gone wrong? Had they really become that useless to the Lord? Were these past years really a waste? What had been motivating them in this work, and how did they lose it?*

What is the basis of a calling? A "calling into missions" should not simply come from a desire to "do something great for God." Nor should it be an escape from a rut or a particular situation. Many have falsely believed that "selling it all and becoming missionaries" can fix problems in their personal, spiritual, and family lives. In fact, it may actually exacerbate them! If they merely follow a "burden for the unreached," they may find themselves in situations for which they and their families were neither called nor gifted. It can be unsafe to operate from a simple feeling such as, "*I do not know why, but I have always had a special place in my heart for Africa*" or "*Since I was a kid, I have always felt as though I'd end up a missionary*" or maybe, "*We do not know why, but we really feel as though God wants us to move overseas.*" We have all read about the exceptions to the rule, but humble wisdom says we should test these feelings and confirm these desires for the sake of our families, our supporters, and the target people.

If we are driven by wrong motivations in life, we cannot expect God's blessing or success.

If we are driven by the wrong motivations in life, we should not expect God's blessing or success. While we may declare our hearts are driven by a passion for God's glory and the worship of His Name throughout the earth, in reality a number of sources can motivate us. As fallen people, we can never have hearts that are 100% purely driven by a godly passion, but we must test our heart motivations. Various problems, even disasters, can occur when we are driven by incorrect desires and misguided enthusiasm. Before we consider overseas ministry, we must be clear on the foundational issue of correct motivations.

When someone comes to a point in their lives when they want to stop living for themselves and serve the living God and His kingdom alone, we rejoice in this heart revival towards the Lord. It is exciting when people declare a new perspective on the world and a new passion for joining in God's mission to the world. These people desire to see repentance and worship from all the peoples of the earth. The last thing we want to do is quench this passion. But if they desire to walk with a pure heart, they must humbly pray, "*Search me, O God, and know my heart! Try me and know my thoughts! And see if there be any grievous way in me, and lead me in the way everlasting*" (Psalm 139:23-24).

Because the heart is "*deceitful above all things*" (Jeremiah 17:9), we need God to help us know the deep motivations of our hearts. Sadly, in every endeavor we pursue, we realize we have a mixture of desires to please ourselves, others, and God. But we press on, clinging to the hope that God's Spirit is leading us, sanctifying us every day, and purifying our desires to make them more like His. We ask God to search us because He alone can "*discern* [our] *thoughts from afar*" and "*search out* [our] *path*" (Psalm 139:2-3). We want Him to search us, so that we are motivated correctly and led in the right direction, at the right pace, and at the right time.

When candidates share with their church and family that they believe the Lord is leading them to pursue cross-cultural ministry overseas, they encounter a variety of responses. Some may rejoice with this step of commitment. Others may be fearful for them. Still others may be surprised by this sudden career change. While some may express their reactions or concerns, most people today seem to believe this "calling" on one's life for a particular vocation is exclusively a personal one. Many believe this calling is often a mystical, spiritual phenomenon. Therefore, unlike other vocational callings, it cannot be challenged or tested in the normal ways.

It is mistakenly assumed that if God has "called this person," then it is not our place to question it. Part of the missionary attrition today, however, is caused by a misunderstanding or doubt regarding calling. Thus many who believe they were called into overseas ministry end up struggling with doubt and confusion once on the field.

Issues of the heart always involve deeply personal and spiritual matters. It can be extremely difficult for people to know without a doubt what their calling is at the present moment. Therefore, we are not suggesting that no one should ever get on an airplane for overseas ministry without a crystal clear calling in his or her heart and mind.

What we *are* suggesting is that in light of the high attrition rates, the deceitfulness of the human heart, and the investment missions candidates are asking others to make to, they should find ways to test their callings for a certain period of time. They should ask the Lord to search their hearts and encourage others to ask them the hard questions. These candidates carry a tremendous weight of responsibility when they ask their family to follow them and their supporters to invest in their callings. No matter how personal, how unique or how spiritual the calling they believe is on their life, as a humble servant of the Lord, they will walk in the light, seek confirmation from older, wiser people and test their callings before God and man.

In life we find that the Lord *leads*, but the Devil *drives*. It is a sad thing to see men or women in overseas ministry being driven every day and, as a result, driving their own families into the ground. Many, fueled by wrong motivations, have become ministry workaholics and have driven others into disasters. We ask how someone with such godly aspirations and commitment to such a godly task *...the Lord leads, the Devil drives.* could fail so miserably on a personal level. One answer lies in motivations. If men and women pursue a godly activity with the wrong impetus, they will not find satisfaction, joy or success in their work.

A man says his passion is to reach the nations, but if in fact he is being driven by a desire to feel significant before God or to please someone else, he follows a dangerous path. A woman declares that her desire is to serve the poor overseas. But if in fact, her deep motivation is to fill a personal emptiness or need for purpose, her decisions can have negative consequences on all involved.

What wrong motivations have led men and women to pursue spiritual exploits on the mission field? Perhaps they are spurred on by spiritual pride or an incorrect theology that believes mission work is the ultimate commitment that pleases God. Some wrongly separate the "secular" and the "spiritual," the "higher calling" from the "mundane calling." They may believe that by going into overseas ministry, they are turning from the world and towards God's work. Throughout church history teachers have been wrongly denigrating workplace spirituality. Eusebius (c. 263 - c. 339) endorsed a spiritual hierarchy, where Christ allows us two ways of life: the *"perfect life,"* available to such spiritual elites as priests and monastics, while the *"permitted life"* is for the rest of us in the ordinary life.[1] The Protestant reformer Martin Luther (1483-1546) sought to correct this unhealthy division by writing, *"The works of monks and priests ... do not differ in the least in the sight of God from the works of the country laborer in the field or a woman going about her household tasks."*[2] We must be careful not to pursue overseas ministry as the highest service to God or most spiritual vocation in life. The gospel gives significance to all work when we do it *"heartily as unto the Lord"* (Colossians 3:23).

Some are driven by an unhealthy idealism that does not take into consideration their giftings, age, spouse, children, and natural limitations. While we are called to ask God for great things and believe Him to accomplish the impossible, He has made each of us with particular giftings and limitations. Instead of viewing these as hindrances or pretending they do not exist, God calls us to know ourselves well, serve according to our giftings, and walk in submission to others. A prideful heart or over-estimation of ourselves can hurt others and keep us from accomplishing the particular work for which God has created us.

...be careful not to pursue overseas ministry as the highest service to God...

So what is the right motivation, the right passion we must ever keep before us to stay healthy in our pursuits, whether they be in banking, architecture or cross-cultural ministry? Our motivation is the Lord Himself. He must be our joy, our passion, our satisfaction, and ultimate fulfillment. His complete forgiveness and acceptance of us must be the foundation of all we do. No "high vocation" or spiritual achievements in life can ever fill that vacuum in our hearts. St. Augustine said it well in his *Confessions*, "*God, you have made us for your-self, and our hearts are restless till they find their rest in you.*"[3] When we begin to strive in our own strength, our own inflated estimation of ourselves, and for our own fulfillment, we can become dangerous misguided missiles that harm others and God's work. Viewing missions as "the ultimate sacrifice" or the most "radical" thing to do with one's life are poor reasons to move overseas. God can lead us to different places in the world to accomplish His particular will for each of us – and moving to a particular place *can* be His will for us – but we must be careful not to fall into the trap of believing that living overseas is the *only* or *best* way to please God or to accomplish something "significant."

How do we keep ourselves in check and make sure our motivations are right and godly? How do we pursue our callings with humility and walk in the light? How can we know if we are being led or driven?

Heart Motivations Checklist:

> Keep God's view of us from His Word before us each day.

> Pray for God to search our hearts and reveal wrong thinking.

> Submit ourselves to older, wiser people and seek their honest input.

> Ask friends to keep a watch out for spiritual pride in us.

> Remember worth is not based on location or vocation.

> Periodically reevaluate what we are doing and what is driving us.

> Make it our goal to serve and empower others.

> Open our lives up to those gifted in counseling.

↪ So, what can we say about checking for right heart motivations in overseas ministry?

Spiritual pride can set a standard neither we nor others can live up to. Working among a people group overseas can be a fulfilling place of ministry, but with the wrong motivations, this work can be a miserable tyrant to serve. *"No one can serve two masters"* (Matthew 6:24). People who are obsessed about being significant make terrible colleagues, spouses, and parents. If deep down we are plagued by a nagging feeling of *"I must keep pushing for that ultimate sacrifice,"* we are in an unhealthy place. We have forgotten that each of us must find our own particular callings and fulfill them, rather than competing to try and do the most momentous thing. Whether we are in the early stages of discovering our calling in life or have been overseas for many years, asking the Holy Spirit

> *Spiritual pride can set a standard neither we nor others can live up to.*

to search our hearts for right motivations and submitting ourselves to others is vital to staying on track. If we are driven by wrong motivations or misguided passions, we may not only fail in our ministry endeavors, we may fail in our most valuable relationships in life. In the end, we may lose everything.

> *"For My people have committed two evils:*
> *They have forsaken Me, the fountain of living waters,*
> *to hew for themselves cisterns, broken cisterns,*
> *that can hold no water."*
> *Jeremiah 2:13*

↪ *The discouraged couple sat on the couch with blank looks on their faces. It was hard to talk about and even harder to pray. How had Alan and Wendy gotten so off track in their hearts and minds? When had they started to focus more on service for the Lord than on the Lord Himself? They were exhausted and burnt out from working so hard to please the Lord with the ultimate sacrifice. All they wanted now was to rest in the Lord's acceptance and grace and learn to walk in it daily. They had discovered how crucial motivation is in life and ministry.*

Discussion Questions (Group or Mentor)

1. What have you learned in your life experiences about the different motivations for going into overseas ministry? Examples?

2. Have you ever seen people wrongly motivated in pursuit of ministry vocations? Did you observe any results?

3. Why do you think people can become obsessed about doing something significant, something radical with their lives?

4. Have you found healthy ways to test your motivations in life?

5. Why are right motivations in overseas ministry so important?

Homework Assignments

Write out your own understanding of your motivations in pursuing cross-cultural ministry overseas. (3-5 pg) Include the following in your paper:

> Why you want to pursue overseas ministry

> How long you have been following this calling

> How you have tested your motivations with experiences and input

> How your calling would be affected if you were never able to go abroad

> Why you believe you are not being driven but led by the Lord

> How you are going to implement the list on page

Chapter 1 Notes

1 David Teague, *Godly Servants: Discipleship and Spiritual Formation for Missionaries* (Mission Imprints, 2012), 56.

2 Martin Luther, *Three Treatises* (Philadelphia: Fortress Press, 1970), 202.

3 Augustine, *Confessions*, trans. Henry Chadwick (Oxford: Oxford University Press, 2008), 3.

Chapter 2

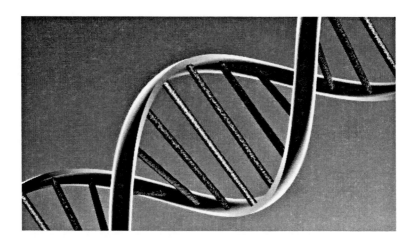

Discovering Personal Giftings

What Is Your Contribution?

"We, though many, are one body in Christ, and individually members one of another. Having gifts that differ according to the grace given to us, let us use them."
Romans 12:5-6

Nathan was a good husband and father of two girls. He had been a successful manager in an engineering company in the U.S. He was known as a faithful servant at his local church. Now he was working for a mission agency, trying to lead a team of young families in how to plant a church in a Muslim country. It had not been easy to go back to school and learn a very foreign language at his age. His personality was struggling with the flexible open-ended schedule each week. It was challenging to adjust to working for weekly goals that were *difficult to measure. Team life involved lots of meetings, social interaction, and one-on-one time with teammates. Nathan was often criticized for his lack of communication and cold approach to tasks. After two years on the mission field, he was having doubts deep inside about whether this vocation was a good fit for him. When he shared them with his wife, Kari, she became fearful about their future and struggled to understand God's leading.*

To be successful in life we must know ourselves well. We should not expect a church or an agency to discover our strengths and giftings for us. We are responsible to pursue that discovery during the course of our lives. Are we currently involved in work and ministry that is enabling us to discover our particular vocational skills and ministry giftings as well as the kinds of work environments that fit us well? Many failures in overseas ministry occur because people enter this particular vocation without enough knowledge of themselves. They have not discovered if their giftings actually fit with living and ministering in a foreign culture using a foreign language. They figure out later on the field that working within a tight community team situation is difficult for them.

Approval by a church or agency is not a stamp of approval from God for cross-cultural, overseas ministry.

Unfortunately, in spite of all the screening interviews, many have found that being approved by a local church or a mission agency does *not* necessarily mean one is fit for or called to cross-cultural living and ministry overseas. Approval by a church or agency is not a stamp of approval from God for cross-cultural, overseas ministry.

We should be proactive to discover our giftings and strengths through trial and error before we commit ourselves to long-term missions service. Acquiring as much experience here at home in the types of work we will most likely be involved in on the field is one of the best ways to discover a work/ministry fit. If we have never built friendships with lost people or been part of a church plant here at home, how can we ask others to support us to do this work in another country and language context? If we have not been engaging the poor or working with kids at risk right here in our hometowns, how can we know about the pitfalls and complicated issues involved? If we don't' do it here, why should we think we can do it 3000 miles away?

Young people today should be encouraged to try different kinds of work and ministries. Youth is a time of discovery. Only rarely do people know in their teens what they are called to do. When we are young, we should say "Yes" to many different jobs and opportunities. Only as we become older should we begin to say "No" to the many options in order to focus on our particular callings. Young people should not be doing the same things and going to the same places every summer, every spring break, every semester.

> *When we are young, we should say "Yes" to many different jobs and opportunities.*

These are times to explore gifts and to discover strengths and weaknesses in ourselves. Is someone interested in helping the poor in India? She should start working with the poor downtown. Is someone interested in reaching Muslims with the gospel? He should get involved with refugees and international students now. Is someone feeling the calling to evangelism/discipleship overseas? He/she should start engaging with the lost and helping new believers grow spiritually here. As we

make mistakes and learn to persevere in challenging relationships, we gain insights about how we can minister overseas.

So, what can we say about personal giftings discovery in regards to overseas ministry?

Moving into a vocation for which we are not gifted can be
detrimental to us and to our families, particularly if it means
moving thousands of miles away. We should be currently
involved with ministry right here at home in order to discover
our own giftings and strengths, especially if we are hoping to
be fruitful in ministry overseas. We should find out what we
have to offer here before we decide to offer it over there. We
can test the waters in a variety of outreach opportunities, jobs,
and study programs. If we are not using our gifts here at home
in English, we are not likely to use them effectively overseas in
another language. We need to see what we have to offer right
here and ask ourselves, *"Are we worthy of export?"*

*As an engineer, Nathan had a desire to engage in God's
mission to reach the nations, and he did not know how to do
that from his small town. He may have understood this desire
to be a "call into overseas missions," when in fact, it may simply
have been the Lord leading him to relocate in the States and
make lifestyle adjustments which would enable him and Kari
to begin to open their home up to internationals in the U.S.
Or it may have been God leading him to use his particular
engineering skills, personality, and giftings in an outreach
center overseas. Nathan should have pursued ways to test his
strengths and giftings in various ministry environments before
he signed up to do very different work.*

Discussion Questions (Group or Mentor)

1. Why is knowing giftings and strengths so important for those wanting to pursue overseas cross-cultural ministry?

2. Why do you believe people think they will do a ministry overseas that they have had little experience with at home?

3. What is the flaw in this kind of thinking, and where does it come from?

4. What kinds of personality and ministry giftings do you think are best for living and working in a cross-cultural environment overseas?

5. What are the best ways to learn your strengths and weaknesses?

Homework Assignments

1. Write out your evaluation of your giftings, strengths, and weaknesses. Explain how these fit into cross-cultural ministry overseas. (3-5 pg) Include the following in your paper:

➤ Experiences that have proven your Christian character through perseverance in difficult relationships

➤ Ministry involvement in the last five years, both formal and informal

➤ Your experience in engaging the lost, both formal and informal

➤ What you have learned about yourself as you attempt to relate cross-culturally and how your gift set fits with cross-cultural ministry

➤ How you have maintained healthy relationships with others

➤ Kinds of work environments in which you thrive and those which are not a good fit for your gifts and personality

2. Take at least *two* of the following TESTS:

> ‣ *DISC Basic Personality Test*: Understand the strengths and challenges of your behavioral style (www.thediscpersonalitytest.com)

> ‣ *Hoozyu* online test: (www.hoozyu.com/app)
> *Hoozyu* is a report package designed to help you make sense of your own motivations and deepest needs and use them to come up with your own menu of options for career and life.

> ‣ *Strengths Finder 2.0* Tom Rath. Omaha, NE: Gallup Press, 2007. (www.strengthsfinder.com) Purchase copy with code.

Chapter 3

Seeking External Confirmation

Do Others Confirm Your Calling?

"Where there is no guidance, a people falls,
but in an abundance of counselors there is safety."
Proverbs 11:14

〜 When Stephen sat down to tell his parents his plans
to move overseas, he did not get the response for which he
was hoping. They asked him about college, jobs, and debt.
Stephen felt his parents lacked spiritual depth and vision. He
had already applied with two different mission agencies who
showed a strong interest in him. Some of his friends were
excited for him, but others had mixed feelings. He used to be
involved with a ministry at church, but a relationship with a
girl during the past year had taken up a lot of time. He had
been through multiple apartments, roommates, and jobs in the

past four years. After attending a global mission conference, he
believed overseas ministry could give him new direction in his
life. He had been on several short-term mission trips with his
church in the past and hoped the church would support him in
this new endeavor.

Ministry is about relationships; no successful minister has ever been a "lone ranger." Healthy people have close friends and mentors who know them well, and they humbly listen to these people and let them speak truth into their lives. True accountability occurs when we submit our lives to older, wiser people who can give us good counsel and insight about ourselves and our particular giftings. Those people who know us well should be able to confirm that our character and giftings fit with a ministry overseas. Even non-Christian parents, bosses, roommates, and teachers can give valuable insight and confirmation in regards to career decisions in our lives.

Those who know us well should be able to confirm that our character and giftings fit with a ministry overseas. Consider these two good questions to ask ourselves:

> ► Can I name some people in my life right now who have been able to watch and evaluate my Christian character, faithfulness in tasks, and ministry gifts in practice here at home over a period of time?

> ► Do these same people confirm that a cross-cultural ministry overseas fits my giftings and my family at this point in my life?

On-field problems commonly issue from a lack of Christian maturity. On-field relational conflicts, moral failures, and insufficient language progress can be related to Christian character. Learning how to operate relationally both at home and with other workers requires humility and forgiveness. Failure to develop personal discipline can make learning a foreign language insurmountable. If we desire to minister overseas, we must develop and exhibit our character at home before others. Character cannot be ascertained through short interviews with a church missions board or even a week-long candidate screening with a mission agency. Self-evaluation is not enough. We need outside confirmation that comes through having close relationships with men and women who understand sound character and what it looks like in daily life. The Apostle Paul writes to Titus that young men should "*in all things show themselves to be an example of good deeds, with purity in doctrine, dignified, sound in speech which is beyond reproach*" (Titus 2:6-8). Regardless of a person's sense of calling, the foundation for achieving long-term effective cross-cultural ministry is true biblical Christian character.

> *...the foundation for achieving long-term effective cross cultural ministry is true biblical Christian character.*

This whole process of gaining confirmation through community maintains integrity in our lives and decisions. We want those who know us best, warts and all, to confirm the big steps in our lives. Why should a mission agency or a church mission board be forced to make decisions based on a limited knowledge of our character, giftings, skills, and family readiness? Before we sit in front of any agency or church board, we should submit ourselves to the confirmation of those who know us best.

*Head and heart confirmation are both important. They
both fit into the category of what many pastors and theologians have described as the internal call. But by themselves they are incomplete. A genuine call to ministry
manifests itself not only in the thoughts and desires of
the called person but also in his gifts, abilities, and skills.
This last aspect of confirmation fits into the category of
what theologians name the external call because it is
the one that is most easily recognizable to other people.[1]*

We want others to confirm that we have the Christian
character needed for succeeding in our relationships and
vocations. Growing sound character involves incorporating
spiritual disciplines into our lives. These are "any activities
through which God works to strengthen our spiritual lives."[2]
Our mentors and close friends help us to start, develop, and
maintain healthy disciplines like Scripture meditation, prayer,
solitude, simplicity, and Sabbath. Have others been able to see
these kinds of habits in our lives on this side of the ocean?

ᔐ So, what can we say about obtaining external confirmation from mentors and friends in regards to our callings and giftings?

Theologian John Calvin wrote, "*Nearly all wisdom we
possess, that is to say, true and sound wisdom, consists
in two parts: the knowledge of God and of ourselves.*"[3]
The best way to learn about ourselves is to ask others to confirm or deny what we believe about our character, strengths,
and weaknesses. Moreover, learning to submit to healthy
accountability *right here* at home is a good sign that someone
will seek out and maintain healthy accountability *over there*!
Such accountability establishes another safe-guard towards
seeing healthy overseas workers and less missionary attrition.
Solomon says, "*Two are better than one, because they have a*

good return for their work: If one falls down, his friend can help him up. But pity the man who falls and has no one to help him up!" (Ecclesiastes 4:9-10 9).

~~~ *Stephen felt like doing something radical in his life, and outreach in Africa looked like the answer. While he definitely needed more purpose and direction in his life, Stephen was asking his church to support this new step. Yet he lacked older men around him, men who knew him and could speak into his life. This young man had not surrounded himself with wise counselors who felt free to speak truth to him, even the hard truth. Was Stephen using missions to escape from responsibilities and missing opportunities to develop his character here at home? Regardless of what the conference speaker had challenged him to do and what the mission agencies had offered, Stephen desperately needed confirmation for these kinds of big decisions in his life. He needs to develop and prove his Christian character over time. Otherwise, he should find a way to support himself with a job overseas as he continues to discover his calling in life.*

Discussion Questions (Group or Mentor)

1. Do you have older wiser people to whom you regularly submit yourself?

2. If not, why not? How can you develop these relationships?

3. Do you think we can ask non-Christian parents, bosses and roommates about our strengths, weaknesses, and decisions?

4. How much time is necessary to evaluate character?

5. How does paying off debt and following through with commitments relate to Christian character?

6. How important do you believe confirmation by a mission board or church committee is in regards to knowing your calling?

Homework Assignments

Write out your present understanding of and experience with healthy accountability and its effect on confirming your calling in life. (3-5 pg) Include the following in your paper:

> Some of your long-standing relationships as mentoree and mentor

> Names of present mentors and their contact information

> Your relationships with your present and past church leadership

> Some long-term missionaries you have met with to discuss your calling

> Important things you have learned about yourself from others

> Anyone who you believe might doubt your calling (Why?)

> Your spouse's and parents' perspective on your ministry gifts and calling

> Your pastor's and mentors' reference letters regarding your calling

Chapter 3 Notes

1 Darrin Patrick, *Church Planter: The Man, the Message, the Mission* (Wheaton: Crossway, 2010), 38.

2 Teague, *Godly Servants*, 71.

3 Jean Calvin, *Institutes of the Christian Religion* (Grand Rapids: Eerdmans, 1995), 15.

Chapter 4

Developing a Cross-Cultural Lifestyle

Are You Engaging Cross-Culturally Now?

"You shall treat the stranger who sojourns with you as the native among you, and you shall love him as yourself."
Leviticus 19:34

Wade and Grace sat across the table from a mission agency representative and began to share how the Muslim world had been on their hearts for several years. Because of college debt, the young couple had been working hard for the past few years. They shared about how they had become interested in this organization's ministry philosophy and overseas opportunities among Muslims. They were pursuing full-time missionary work with this group. They had only been on short-term mission trips but had no real experience in working with Muslims. Their present jobs had very little to do with what they *desired to do overseas. The mission agency was laying out for them the steps to joining the organization, choosing a country, and raising support. Wade and Grace decided they would start praying over a map of the Muslim world.*

Following a romanticized view of "overseas missionary work" is a dangerous path and can lead to disappointment and serious ramifications for us, our families, and even our faith. Overseas cross-cultural ministry should not be seen as a career change that one can simply "learn on the job" with hard work after arriving in a foreign country. Many testify to having some sort of initial "spiritual calling into missions," which may just be a willingness to go anywhere the Lord leads. Experience shows we should, however, do all we can to see this "calling" both tested over time and confirmed through various experiences before making a decision to move a family overseas.

Let's be clear about what we mean by "calling." Os Guinness, in his seminal work *The Call*, gives us a helpful understanding of calling. As a follower of Christ, my primary calling is to God, first and foremost. My secondary calling is to a vocation, a line of work, which is something for which God has given me special talents and desires, such as engineering, medicine, administration, teaching, or counseling. Guinness says I fulfill

> *Following a romanticized view of overseas missionary work is a dangerous path...*

my secondary calling with my primary calling always in focus.[1] So we are called to God *and* to a vocation, both of which can be fulfilled in a variety of venues. When we speak of a "calling to missions," like any other vocation, we are actually saying that we believe God has uniquely gifted and designed us to minister in a cross-cultural context. How can we know we have been designed for this vocation?

Lasting kingdom impact within a culture requires understanding how to relate cross-culturally. If we don't have experience in cross-cultural relationships, we will be unprepared for adaptation and penetration into a culture. This endeavor wastes time, energy, and money in a ministry about which we know nothing and to which we were never called. Not every believer is called to and gifted for cross-cultural evangelism/discipleship. Moreover, language aptitude, age, family size, and cross-cultural skills all affect our ability to acculturate, thrive, learn a language well and be effective in a cross-cultural environment overseas.

False expectations and glorified concepts regarding "taking the gospel to the unreached" have drawn many overseas.

In general, those who immerse themselves in cross-cultural ministry at home are the most successful in overseas living and ministry. Many of them also studied or worked abroad for a year to immerse themselves in a cross-cultural lifestyle. Americans sometimes falsely imagine that after arriving on their new mission field, they will have the ability and desire to "jump into cross-cultural life" and adapt themselves to it. This is dangerous thinking. False expectations and glorified concepts regarding "taking the gospel to the unreached" have drawn many overseas. Unfortunately, many have found living and relating cross-culturally much more difficult than they had expected.

Finally, integrating our calling to cross-cultural ministry here and preparing ourselves for overseas living will require lifestyle changes now. Moving overseas will bring a loss of many of the support systems and conveniences on which we have become dependent. Those who want to test and prepare themselves for overseas living might consider making life-style choices similar to what they will experience in a foreign country, such as moving into a small apartment in their city. Learning to live more simply, developing fewer but closer friends, gathering for worship in a home setting, practicing hospitality, and shopping locally can be beneficial, particularly for families. Couples with children are often not prepared for the huge loss they experience when they no longer have grandparents, youth programs, organized activities, church support, and friends close by.

Seeing the Mission Fields Around Us

Richard Bailey in his insightful article "Who's Turning the Mission Field Upside Down?" writes that, "*God is moving people around today in what may be the greatest migration the world has ever seen, and his purpose is that these people may find the light of his salvation through Jesus Christ.*"[2] Bailey explains how God in His sovereign plan is using:

> religious and civil revolutions

> natural disasters, drought, disease

> economic and political upheavals

> educational and employment opportunities

> globalization of economics and media

in order to...

> break down geopolitical boundaries set up by governments

> open up countries that are closed to traditional mission outreach

> scatter peoples to every corner of the earth...

"so that men would seek Him and perhaps reach out for Him" (Acts 17:27).

The Church can be influenced by the world and must constantly realign itself with the worldview laid out in Scripture. Many in the Church today believe global missions is only about foreign countries and missionary work is about getting on an airplane. In reality missions is about ethnic groups, not countries, and missionary work is about reaching people groups. People ask, "*Where* are you going to serve?" But the more biblical question would be, "*Whom* are you going to serve?" Traditionally, we have targeted seven continents, roughly 195 geopolitical countries, lands with borders, but we must instead focus on the 16,000 to 24,000 different ethno-linguistic groups of the world, wherever they may be living. For example, if we tell people we are going to work among Turkish people, most would think we are heading for the country of Turkey. Actually, several million Turks live in Europe, and thousands are studying and working in the U.S. and around the world.

Missions is about ethnic groups, not countries...

We used to assume, when someone said they were called to be a missionary, that they were headed to another *country*. Today, a missionary goes to work among a people group, *wherever* they live. Today, reaching the Punjabi people could mean either going to the country of Pakistan or India or going to work among the millions of Punjabi people living in the UK. Bailey says we used to think geographic proximity determined the availability of the gospel, i.e., the more remote the place, the more urgent the need. But he explains that now we see how cultural and linguistic proximity determines access to the gospel much more than geography. Therefore, the greater the linguistic and cultural "distance," the more urgent the need. Sometimes a huge population of refugees lives in the shadow of U.S. churches, yet they are linguistically and culturally "far away" from the gospel. This same church may even be sending missionaries to those very refugees' home country. God has unreached peoples living down the street from us right here in the U.S.

We need new eyes to see the new mission fields God is establishing. In times past we thought we could reach a people group only by living in their homeland. Today we find we can reach them by living among them, whether they are in their heartland or among a *diaspora* of refugees or immigrants living in a different part of the world. God is at work in the world, shaking countries up, scattering peoples of the world to every corner of the globe. Geopolitical and water boundaries are not crucially important in missions anymore. We have to ask whether a mono-cultural outreach approach even constitutes an option in today's multicultural world. God is calling His Church to embrace this unique period of time for decision and action in history, and to step out to reach the nations living right in our own cities.

A short-term missions trip can greatly expand our heart and mind to God's great global purpose in the world. But cross-cultural missions exposure and experience no longer requires spending a lot of money to go overseas. We can bring the gospel to unreached people groups who live right in our cities. Ethnic concentrations in the United States are expanding every day.[3] What should our response be to the high numbers of refugees, students, and immigrants coming into the U.S.? Can we slow it down, stop it, restrict it? While some of us can and should be involved in seeing better filtering in the immigration process, we need to focus more on our attitudes and behavior towards these internationals. Perhaps immigration is one way in which God has sovereignly chosen to bring the peoples of the world closer to the gospel. Since the Church has not been faithful in going to the unreached around the world, perhaps God has chosen to bring them to our doorsteps.

Many families today have found it too difficult to uproot their families, drop their present responsibilities at home and secure the expected financial support for overseas mission work. These families, however, have discovered new "mission fields" they had never seen before. They are engaging with refugees, students, and immigrants in their city on a regular basis. They have also discovered that this kind of outreach is not only doable for them, but it is also quite strategic for reaching Muslims, Buddhists, and Hindus.

Immigration is one way in which God has sovereignly chosen to bring the peoples of the world closer to the gospel.

If we have not been involved in cross-cultural evangelism and discipleship among internationals in our home communities, how can we be sent out to do evangelism and discipleship in a more difficult foreign language context? We should have integrity in our lives, with our talk being reflected in our walk. Christian character should always supersede any supposed callings, burdens for a people group or ministry vision. A plane ticket overseas does not change who we are. We can begin to integrate our calling to cross-cultural ministry by building relationships with internationals in our home cities. A passion for and gifting in cross-cultural ministry should be visible in us before we move our family into a third-world city 3000 miles away.

In today's multicultural world, it seems strange to send people to reach Muslims overseas who have not taken the time to develop friendships with Muslims during their years of preparation for missions service. Does this suggest a bit of arrogance and Western over-confidence? The Lord of the harvest has given a perfect pre-field testing ground right here in our communities. Let us not be blind to the incredible opportunities all around because of "*an erroneous idea that 'missions'*

*is something that occurs overseas, not in [our] hometowns."*4
Sustained involvement in cross-cultural relationships now is
the best way to confirm a calling and start our training.

ᕼ So, what can we say about the need for developing a cross-cultural lifestyle right now?

A desire to be involved with overseas cross-cultural ministry
often begins with a spiritual experience in the heart, a surren-
dering of life plans to God. This desire, however, always grows
and develops over time and should begin to direct our lives
and the lifestyle choices we make. High levels of migration
in the world today leave no excuse for any candidate not to
be building friendships and ministering cross-culturally to
internationals right at home. If we believe we are called to
long-term overseas ministry, we should test this calling and
take advantage of all the opportunities available to develop our
cross-cultural skills. Moreover, Westerners are rarely prepared
for daily life in the new culture, the loss of conveniences, and
the local community lifestyle. We must begin now to make
important choices to test and prepare ourselves for the typical
lifestyle of overseas living. Basically, we need to know and live
our callings here before we take them over there. We want
to be people who are "worthy of hire" in regards to ministry
support by making sure our callings are integrated with our
present ministry and lifestyles (1 Timothy 5:18). Those who
want to become astronauts, first start flying airplanes, then
proceed to rockets!

Training Courses for working among Muslims in the U.S.
1. *Encountering The World of Islam*
   (www.encounteringislam.org)
2. *Bridges: Christians Connecting With Muslims.*
   (www.crescentproject.org)

Outreach Ministries to Internationals in the U.S.
1. World Relief Refugee Services
   (www.worldrelief.org)
2. Bridges International Student Outreach
   (www.bridgesinternational.com)
3. International Students Inc.
   (www.isionline.org)

Search the web for the local outreach ministries in your area. It would, however, be better simply to begin to observe your own community, where you work, go to school, and shop. There are so many internationals living around us; we are often just too busy to notice and engage them.

Wade and Grace needed guidance at the local church level. They needed older people who could counsel them in the different ways to discover and test their callings right here among internationals at home. They did not need an agency putting a map in front of them to pick a place to serve. Wade and Grace need to put their burden for Muslims into action and start living their calling now. They need to start having Muslims into their home and begin to learn how to befriend and witness to them. They should also begin to make lifestyle changes that prepare them for overseas living.

Discussion Questions (Group or Mentor)

1. Is cross-cultural ministry a vocation anyone can become effective in overseas if they are willing to move there and work hard at it? Explain.

2. What are some signs that someone is gifted for cross-cultural ministry?

3. In what ways can someone fulfill a calling to cross-cultural ministry without ever moving overseas?

4. What are the benefits of making friendships with internationals here?

5. What are some benefits to living and working overseas for a year prior to pursuing long-term cross-cultural ministry?

6. What are the benefits to a one-year self-supporting job overseas?

7. What kinds of pre-field life experiences would help someone be successful in living and ministering cross-culturally overseas?

Homework Assignments

Write out your understanding of your calling and how it has affected your lifestyle and ministry here. (3-5 pg) Include the following in your paper:

> Articulate your vocational calling into overseas cross-cultural ministry, when it started and how it has grown over time.

> How this calling has changed the way you live and serve here

> How what you will do over there fits with who you are and what you have been doing

> How this calling involves moving to another country

> Experiences in interacting in a cross-cultural environment over the past few years (overseas or at home) and what you learned

- Relationships you have developed among internationals in your community and ministries in your city

- Research findings about international population in your area and the particular ministries engaging these internationals

- Lifestyle changes you have made to test and equip yourself and your family for overseas living situations and local community environments

Chapter 4 Notes

1   Os Guinness, *The Call: Finding and Fulfilling the Central Purpose of Your Life* (Nashville: W Publishing Group, 2003), 31.

2   Richard P. Bailey, "Who's Turning the Mission Field Upside Down?," *Evangelical Missions Quarterly* 37, no.1 (Jan. 2001), 52.

3   "USA Right Now," http://www.usarightnow.com (Accessed August 12, 2013)

4   Joshua Massey, "Hometown Ministry as Pre-field Preparation," *Evangelical Missions Quarterly* 38 (April 2002), 197.

Chapter 5

Obtaining a Marketable Expertise

Do You Need More Education?

"...they were tentmakers by trade."
Acts 18:3

~ *Jay and Kelli were in their early twenties. His degree was in philosophy, but he was not quite sure how he could use it in a vocation. Kelli had studied interior decorating in college. At present they were working in coffee shops and retail stores. Their interest in overseas living and ministry started with college mission trips. They had been researching a few mission agencies. The particular area of the world in which they were interested did not allow for missionary visas, so one organization used student visas as an entry strategy. They knew this would work for a while but was not a long-term solution to staying in-country. With their degrees and experience they could not obtain employment in the country. Jay did not think they could raise the large amount of support being proposed by the mission groups. Kelli was not comfortable asking their church and friends to support them in this new venture. Their present jobs were not enabling them to save much money. They had a desire to go but felt stuck in their present situation.*

In today's economy, many churches and mission organizations are witnessing a decrease in financial support on a global scale. This decline in giving is affecting their abilities to send out full-time mission workers. Missionaries on the field are experiencing financial struggles like never before. It is becoming more difficult for those pursuing full-time missionary work to raise the huge amounts of support that agencies are expecting. These changes have made us consider new ways of entering countries and supporting cross-cultural workers overseas.

Churches, organizations, and candidates today must recognize the economic realities in the world and embrace new strategies. This paradigm shift does not have to be viewed in a negative light. The Lord of the Harvest wants us simply to become more creative in finding economical ways of launching His workers into fields around the world. Moreover, asking this new generation to become more self-supporting in their overseas ministry endeavors is not just about economics—it is missiologically strategic.

Most of the countries where the least reached peoples of the world live are closed to a traditional missionary visa status and require us to have some kind of vocational platform to establish residence. Fake "cover jobs" often bring frustration and may create suspicion among those with whom we are engaging. Paul did not use his right to support but said he would *"endure all things lest [he] hinder the gospel of Christ"* (1 Corinthians 9:12). Because of U.S. political and military involvement around the globe, Westerners are finding it more difficult to live overseas without creating suspicion and distrust. When we enter a country to serve a people, using our skills in a tangible way, we are appreciated and trusted more easily. A genuine job platform which serves the target community can help establish an authentic presence within a country and produce a better model for locals as well. Instead of hindering one's ministry, a job can actually give more natural opportunities for language learning and culture assimilation.

While we may have a clear job description and vocational position as a "missionary" from a home church and an agency perspective, the local society we are entering may struggle to understand and accept our presence among them. Have we considered how locals around the world view foreigners today, particularly Westerners, who live in their countries? Would it be a wise plan to get further education *When we enter a country to serve a people, using our skills in a tangible way, we are appreciated and trusted more easily.* to obtain a marketable skill which could give us a bona fide job platform overseas? A job in-country can not only establish residency but can create a legitimate presence in the new society, provide a way for building natural relationships, and enable us to be more self-supporting.

When we acquire the proper education and vocational experience before heading overseas, we will also gain valuable life skills needed to be successful in serving in another country. Though we might assume such skills have already been developed, agencies and field staff are discovering that many new candidates lack basic life skills in areas such as responsible and independent living, healthy work and study habits, handling money and resources, time management, social skills, personal discipline, and health habits. If we have not developed these life skills, we cannot expect to have the discipline for healthy work and study habits needed to master a language. We cannot hope to maintain good communication with those on the field and at home, submit to authority or work in a team environment. It is definitely a great idea for those pursuing overseas ministry first to have a few years of real life experience in independent living and normal work before leaving for the field. We should never see preparing for overseas cross-cultural living and ministry simply as a matter of spirituality and theology. Part of spiritual maturity involves developing practical life skills for managing ourselves, our families, and our work/ministry.

Many new candidates lack basic life skills in responsible and independent living, healthy work and study habits, personal discipline...

Finally, having a marketable expertise can help candidates engage with the lost and internationals in their home countries as they prepare for overseas ministry. At the same time, these skills can provide needed income while waiting to leave as well as be a practical benefit if they have to return home unexpectedly. Many have used their vocational skills to obtain a job and support themselves overseas, allowing churches to use their resources to support outreach projects. Like the Apostle Paul they have chosen to be "tentmakers" and *"toil and labor night and day, that [they] might not be a burden"* to the Church (2 Thessalonians 3:18). Bottom line, getting a marketable skill today is both strategic and wise.

Acquiring Cross-Cultural Experience Overseas

Am I called to cross-cultural ministry? Is a spiritual "call" to missions enough to legitimize one's gaining approval and training to become a long-term cross-cultural worker? Many Christians desire to be involved with cross-cultural ministry overseas but do not know what that would look like long-term. Most of the options before them involve raising a large amount of financial support. While mission agencies are willing to accept couples for overseas ministry, some candidates do not feel ready or comfortable with the "full-time missionary" vocation process. What they really need is *What they really need is is some on-the-ground experience in cross-cultural living and ministry for an extended period of time.* some on-the-ground experience in cross-cultural living and ministry for an extended period of time. Having a marketable expertise can open a door to *"go and explore the land"* (Judges 18:2).

With all the global job opportunities, many are finding a better option for getting exposure to cross-cultural living and ministry by obtaining a job overseas for a couple of years. College graduates can get degrees or certificates which enable them to obtain jobs overseas using a marketable skill. Teaching English is one of the best ways to have an all-expense-paid one- or two-year overseas experience. A person can attend a one month or summer TEFL (Teaching English as Foreign Language) Certificate program at a local university or online and then apply for TEFL jobs via the Internet or contacts overseas. Many institutions will pay for airfare and housing as well as do all the work visa documentation. While teaching abroad is the most common job, most of us are unaware of the variety of overseas jobs available today. Many young people are spending a year overseas coaching a sport, doing research, being a nanny, serving in a hospital, or working on an organic farm. Such a job will allow them to live and work overseas for one or two years and get a clearer picture of cross-cultural living, language learning, and long-term ministry overseas. It will also enable them to interact with long-term foreign workers there and learn from the national believers in the country regarding the real needs and benefits of foreign mission work.

The Apostle Paul used his occupation as a tentmaker during his missionary journeys to earn his livelihood as well as to establish gospel integrity (Acts 18:3; 1 Corinthians 9:12). Missional tentmakers are Christians who use their marketable skills to obtain employment overseas. Sometimes tent making enables them to enter a "restricted country," i.e., a country closed to traditional mission work. In other cases, they may want simply to avoid having an identity as a "full-time professional religious worker." Missional tent making is about the sacredness of all work, the priesthood of the believer, over-coming local bias, the power of witness through work, and the importance of modeling lifestyle ministry to young believers and immature churches.[1] It is about providing foreign visitors with a base of integration into a community and being a witness to influential persons in that town, something that may be difficult to achieve as regular missionaries.

Missional tentmaking is about the sacredness of all work, the priesthood of the believer, the power of witness through work, and modeling lifestyle...

The Church today needs an urgent wake-up call to the fact that a large-scale movement of missional marketplace witnesses is the only strategy that will enable the church to carry out the Great Commission in many countries in the world. Bottom line, individuals and churches are learning that more effective and even cheaper options than typical short-term mission trips are available to help people grasp the nature of overseas living, understand the task of cross-cultural ministry, and discover the best ways to fit into God's global mission.

⟳ So, what can we say about having the marketable skills to establish a legitimate profession overseas?

Due to the present economic crisis, the available funds are insufficient for sending all the candidates desiring to go overseas. Moreover, in this post-9/11 world, Westerners are finding it harder to enter many countries, establish residence, and create rapport with locals overseas. If our goal is to enter a society for the purpose of serving locals and establishing authentic relationships of trust, we may need further education and a global marketable skill to have a bona fide platform. It is best to have this kind of vocational training, degree, or related work experience completed *prior* to leaving for the field. Adding to this education, a couple of years of work in the marketplace will also develop the healthy life skills needed for the task at hand. This marketable expertise also opens doors for spending an extended period of time overseas to experience real life and work in a cross-cultural environment.

⟳ If Jay and Kelli had obtained globally marketable skills during college, these could have enabled them to secure jobs in the region of the world in which they were interested. In fact, they could have already been overseas. The best plan right now may be to pursue a certificate or graduate degree. With a TEFL Certificate, they could get a paying job overseas. They could also pursue work with overseas international schools. These kinds of jobs could at least get Jay and Kelli over there and give them a chance to test their callings for a year.

Recommended Resources

www.tentmakernet.com

www.tentmakersinternational.info

www.globalopps.org

www.worldwidetentmakers.com

www.tesol.org

www.tefl.com

www.itnuk.com

www.cambridgeenglish.org/exams-and-qualifications/celta

www.workasworshipnetwork.org

www.businessasmission.com

www.lausanne.org/en/connect/topics/business-as-mission.html

www.nics.org - Network of International Christian Schools

Discussion Questions (Group or Mentor)

1. How do you think locals' view of foreigners living in their countries has changed in the last 10-15 years?

2. What do you think are the benefits of bona fide platform jobs overseas?

3. Do you think a job could hinder language study and cultural adaptation?

4. What do you think about the time and money necessary to establish and run a successful business overseas for the purpose of platform?

5. What do you believe would be the greatest challenges in establishing an identity and an entry platform in a society overseas?

6. What are the benefits of someone first working in a secular job in his/her own country before pursuing missions overseas?

7. Do you think someone getting training and experience in a marketable skill shows a lack of faith in a spiritual calling to cross-cultural ministry?

8. Why is real life experience in independent living and normal work before leaving for the field important?

Homework Assignments

Write down your present vocational marketable expertise. (3-5 pg) Include the following in your paper:

> Your marketable skills/degrees for obtaining work overseas

> Research about the visa requirements, job options, and working conditions in a particular country in which you are interested

> Research about three ways to get further education/ qualifications in a skill, including a certificate or degree such as ESL/EFL teaching

- ▸ A feasible society entry plan, including how your background and education could fit with this job description

- ▸ Lessons from three people who have done similar platform jobs in an area of the world in which you are interested

- ▸ Advice from three people with overseas experience regarding the benefits of developing real life skills before going overseas

- ▸ The practical life and work experiences you have had to develop your life skills which will help you in responsible living, personal discipline, submission to authority, and healthy relationships

Chapter 5 Notes

1   Jonathan Lewis, "Taking Tentmaking Beyond Mutually Exclusive Definitions" (World Evangelical Alliance Resources, 2006) www.worldevangelicals.org/resources/rfiles/res3_56_link_1283199525.pdf (Accessed August 8, 2013)

Part I Action List
The PERSON

☐ **1. Check Heart Motivations**
Ask the Lord to search your heart as well as submit yourself to others to make sure you are being led by the Lord and not being driven by unhealthy or wrong motivations for pursuing overseas ministry.

☐ **2. Discover Personal Giftings**
Actively pursue ministries, jobs, courses, and experiences that can help you discover your strengths, giftings, and ideal work/ministry environments as well as equip you for your future work/ministry.

☐ **3. Seek Out External Confirmation**
Surround yourself with older, wiser people to whom you can regularly submit your character development, ministry calling, and career decisions over a period of time.

☐ **4. Begin a Cross-Cultural Lifestyle**
Start living out your calling to cross-cultural ministry by developing friendships among the international community in your city, and make some practical lifestyle changes to prepare yourself for overseas.

☐ **5. Obtain a Marketable Expertise**
Acquire training and experience in a marketable skill in order to gain important life skills now, create a genuine platform for relationships overseas, and provide a way to support yourself overseas.

Part I Further Reading
The PERSON

The Call: Finding and Fulfilling the Central Purpose of Your Life. Os Guinness. Nashville: W Pub. Group, 2003.

Live Your Calling: A Practical Guide to Finding and Fulfilling Your Mission in Life. Kevin & Kay Marie Brennfleck. San Francisco: Jossey-Bass, 2005. (www.liveyourcalling.com)

Discovering God's Will: How to Make Every Decision with Peace and Confidence. Jerry Sittser. Grand Rapids: Zondervan, 2002.

Connecting: The Mentoring Relationships You Need to Succeed in Life. Paul D. Stanley and Robert Clinton. Colorado Springs: Navpress, 1992.

Cultural Intelligence: Improving Your CQ to Engage Our Multicultural World. David A. Livermore. Grand Rapids: Baker Academic, 2009.

The Journey of a Post-modern Missionary: Finding One's Niche in Cross-cultural Ministry. Richard Glenn Lewis. Longwood: Xulon Press, 2006.

Part II

The PARTNERS

After passing the preliminary screening at NASA,
one can enter astronaut candidate training.
A vital part of that preparation is understanding
the roles of the key partners in the mission,
those on the ground at base command
and those in the air, the flight crew.

In a similar way, when considering an extended
period of overseas ministry, what are the critical
questions to ask regarding the key PARTNERS
we will need in this mission,
both at home and abroad?

Chapter 6

Considering Family Needs

*How Will You Equip
And Protect Your Family?*

*"But if anyone does not provide for his own,
and especially for those of his household,
he has denied the faith, and is worse than an unbeliever."*
1 Timothy 5:8

⁓ Caleb and Molly had been living overseas for three years. She had never wanted to homeschool the children, but was willing to try it for the sake of the mission. Having two young children and a new baby made it difficult to get out and learn the new language well. Her lack of language mastery limited her ability to make friendships with neighbors and women in the community. Molly was feeling isolated and alone at home. The occasional visit from teammates was not *enough to meet her social needs. On the other hand, Caleb was progressing quickly, enjoying his days of language learning and building new relationships. Tensions between them began to rise when other team members started to make comments about how little Molly was progressing and engaging with society. It all came to a head when the team leader's wife confronted Molly about her lack of ministry involvement. That night, she broke down with Caleb, sharing how much pressure she felt to accomplish everything on her plate. Caleb was living his dream; Molly was drowning.*

When a couple considers overseas cross-cultural ministry, it is important to discover the source of the original call. Did this call begin with the husband or the wife? One should be careful that the spouse is more than just "willing to go" and not feeling "pulled along" in this process. Cross-cultural living and ministry is usually twice as hard on a wife as on a husband. Many have confessed they were unprepared for how difficult it was to lose family, church, friends, and the practical helps found in Western societies.

Sometimes the wife assumes she will be involved with her husband's work in the way she has been at home in the West. Wives can under-estimate the level of language mastery they will need to run a home, accomplish daily tasks, and practice hospitality in a community-based culture. In some cultures, there is social segregation and women interact only with other women. A woman who goes overseas with small children may struggle to achieve language competency. To focus on language learning in the early years, she will need funds to hire house help and childcare. If she is also attempting to homeschool children, her time will be even more limited. If a wife does not learn the language well, she can fail to assimilate with the culture and stop engaging with the people. Her lack of success in these areas may lead to detachment from the society. If a husband is progressing and the wife and children are not, marriage tensions can rise.

Before a decision is made to move overseas, a wife should be proactive in contacting and inter-acting with other mothers living in the target country about all the issues in raising and educating children in that country. Children's lack of adjustment, education, or friendship opportunities can often cause people

Wives assume they will be involved with their husband's work in the ways they have been at home in the West.

to leave the field early. Let's ask a few questions about children:

> Have your children ever had to play with and befriend other children who do not speak English well?

> Have you and your children ever been in a continuous situation where they must daily interact with non-Christian children whose worldviews, standards of right and wrong, and view of authority are radically different from your own?

> Are you prepared for your children to grow up in an environment where they have very few Christian friends?

> Have you interviewed long-term missionary families to learn about the issues involved with raising and educating children in a foreign culture?

When evaluating a couple's calling to overseas cross-cultural ministry, husbands and churches may underemphasize the wife's personality and giftedness for this kind of work. Focusing so much on the husband's giftings and preparedness ignores how much of a partner in ministry the wife will have to be in most community-oriented or "hot" cultures. We should ask the wife a few questions:

> ➤ What do you see as the primary goals in the first three years for you and your children in the areas of language learning and ministry?

> ➤ Do you believe these expectations fit with those of your husband, church, and if applicable at present, mission agency/team?

> ➤ Do you believe you need the same calling as your husband for this work?

> ➤ Have you had ample time to test your personality and giftings in cross-cultural outreach in your own country?

> ➤ Have you developed good time-management skills and personal discipline in order to be able to fulfill home responsibilities overseas and then add the extra hours needed to learn a foreign language?

It is critical for a man, his wife, his church, and his agency to have the same expectations regarding his wife and children in the new environment. They should research the cost of house help and childcare to enable the wife to get out, go to classes, and learn the language.

It is critical to make sure a man, his wife, his church, and his agency are on the same page regarding expectations...

Another important family factor to consider in the early years is the use of English. While English-speaking friendships and ministries can meet social needs during the adjustment period, over time these kinds of ministries can become a distraction and even a hindrance to a family's acculturating, learning the language, and bonding with the local people and culture.

If a couple agrees to move overseas, they need to do all the research they can before going. They should obtain counsel from those with experience in family life overseas as well as develop a system of healthy accountability. As time passes on the field, it is not the wife, the team or the agency, but the husband who carries the weight of responsibility to respond wisely if he sees that his wife and children are not thriving. We must be totally frank here: if a husband does not protect and care for his wife and kids overseas, he may not only lose his ministry, but in the long run, he

> *If a husband does not protect his wife and kids overseas, he may not only lose his ministry, he may lose his family as well.*

may lose his family as well. Let's ask the husband a few important questions:

> ➤ What are your realistic expectations for your wife and children regarding language learning and ministry for the first years and after that period?

> ➤ Who is responsible for your family having what they need to survive and thrive in this new place?

> ➤ Do you have healthy accountability relationships at present, and what is your plan to have these in place overseas?

In years past, a husband with a calling was deemed sufficient for a wife to pack up and follow him to the jungle. Today, however, many families seem unaware of and less prepared for the challenges of maintaining a home and raising and educating children in foreign lands.

Let's be clear: many families *are* successfully acculturating among unreached peoples, thriving overseas, and making an impact today. We simply want every family to be fully aware of the challenges in order to make wise decisions. Families that do well make difficult but wise decisions regarding lifestyle and commit themselves to focus solely on language and culture before anything else. One of the keys to a wife/mother being able to function, minister, and enjoy living overseas is gaining language fluency.

Considering Older Couples

Missionaries in the past used to arrive on the field as young singles or young married couples. Today's missionary candidates are becoming burdened about the unreached of the world later in life. The current trend is to send out couples in their 30's and 40's (with children) into closed pioneer fields. They are given the task of learning a language, educating their children, doing effective evangelism and discipleship, running a platform business, and facilitating a church plant. Often the candidates and their churches are not fully aware of the tasks a typical family must do to survive, thrive, and be effective in a cross-cultural environment overseas.

Statistics show that men in their mid-30's or older struggle to learn languages spoken among the unreached people groups of the world. These men's wives struggle even more to achieve a language level needed to fully adapt and minister effectively via hospitality, family gatherings, and ministry activities. While the husband is out learning the language, the wife is struggling to learn to cook in the new culture, homeschool children, and fulfill daily needs for the family as well as fit time in for language lessons.

Although established mission fields generally have more developed language programs and missionary schools, pioneer fields often do not. Thus the burden of language/culture learning falls on the individual. When their language level "fossilizes," they may slide towards doing English-based ministries, attending international churches, and just surviving as ex-pats.

While many couples with children *do succeed* entering a new culture, learning a difficult language well, and making an effective impact, mission mobilizers should make sure these older candidates are prepared for the tasks before them. We see in Scripture and throughout church history that God uses godly men and women of all ages in His Kingdom work.

Although each of us in the Church *can* fit somewhere in reaching the nations, not everyone is capable of doing every kind of ministry in every setting. For this reason, local churches should be more pro-active to challenge, mentor, and equip college students, singles, and young couples for cross-cultural ministry overseas. They should encourage them to engage with internationals at home as well as spend a year overseas ministering cross-culturally. True servants who desire to reach the nations and serve according to their God-given abilities should be willing to work with unreached peoples in whatever context the Lord provides, whether in their own city or abroad.

> *Mission mobilizers should make sure older candidates clearly understand and are prepared for the tasks before them.*

In fact, what newly forming churches around the world particularly need are older, mature men and women to teach and model Christian character and family life. In many cultures in the world, older people are shown instant respect simply because of age. So while our focus is to mobilize and equip young people to go overseas, the goal is to see these young men and women stay on the field, learn the language and culture, and become effective ministers for many years.

✆ So, what can we say about these essential considerations when taking a family to live and work overseas?

A couple should do all the research they can and submit themselves to the wisdom of those with years of experience in regards to the decisions they make and the particular field to which they go. Once again, working with internationals here at home for a couple of years would be a wise way to test a marriage and family in cross-cultural ministry. Bottom line, your most important mission partner is your family. A wife needs to know herself, her calling, her limits and the expectations on her. A husband needs to make sure his wife and children know clearly what he, the mission team and the home church expect from them. Clearly defined expectations alone can greatly reduce missionary attrition today and give them success overseas.

Caleb and Molly should have interviewed other families regarding the realities of doing cross-cultural ministry while raising a family overseas. Being overly idealistic about what a mother of three can accomplish in the early years was not wise. Caleb and Molly could have been clearer on their goals and expectations with each other prior to going. Then, with their own unified plan and expectations, they could have verbalized these to their church, agency, and team. Caleb and Molly could have left with a clearer understanding of the task before them. Instead, Caleb must now make some hard decisions on the field about how to help Molly succeed there.

Discussion Questions (Group or Mentor)

1. Should a wife have her own calling to overseas ministry?

2. If not, what should her commitment level be to the ministry?

3. What do you believe are the key components for ensuring that a man prioritizes and protects his marriage and family overseas?

4. How could a wife or husband find herself/himself feeling trapped in ministry overseas?

5. Why do you think it's harder for a woman living overseas?

6. What role should age and family size play in determining a move overseas?

7. How important is it to have children on board with your calling?

8. What are the pros and cons of English-based friendships and ministries?

Homework Assignments

Both husband and wife write out their understandings of their callings and how they fit with each others' roles in this work. (2-3 pg) The following should be included in their papers:

> Background, personality, and giftings in the work he/she will do

> Realistic expectations and key goals for each family member for the first three years in the areas of language learning and ministry

> Funding plan to enable wife and children to focus on the language

> Plan to ensure that their expectations fit with each other's as well as those of the local church, on-field team, and agency

> Steps to take when someone in the family is not thriving overseas

> Past experiences when either the husband or wife put ministry/work above family needs and what was learned

> Findings from interviews with 2-3 missionaries about the challenges a wife and children can expect when living in the target country

> Lessons they learned regarding how some thrived and some failed

> Answers to the 12 questions asked within the chapter to husband and wife about children and expectations.

Chapter 7

Maintaining Strong Relationships at Home

Do You Have Close Friends In Your Home Church?

"A friend loves at all times,
and a brother is born for adversity."
Proverbs 17:17

~ Jamie and Deb had been serving for six years at a Christian hospital overseas. Their language level was developing well and ministry to the local people was quite fulfilling. The most difficult issues they were facing involved the co-worker community at the hospital. Over the last two years there had been many changes and conflicts within the leadership. Weekly meetings had become tense and awkward. Their own organizational leadership and teammates were all *part of the hospital, and no one seemed to have the courage needed to pursue resolution. Jamie and Deb were concerned about the spiritual conditions at the hospital and how it was affecting them. They needed counsel but were not sure how to proceed.*

Unless we have ever moved overseas for a period of time and left behind everything and everybody we know, it is hard to understand the loss and loneliness of overseas ministry. If we move to another city, we have to cultivate new friendships and connect to our new community. When we move overseas the Christian community is often smaller and quite different from the ones back home. We also encounter new challenges caused by transportation, mission organizational lines, team leadership styles, teammate dynamics, and the new foreign culture. Good relationships will be key to adjusting and thriving in the new environment.

We will enhance our chances of success by embracing the responsibility of nurturing close friendships within our church back home.

Our goal is to establish a new home with new friends. Our goal is *not* to lean on our relationships back home, thousands of miles away. In fact, developing close friendships with locals in the community will be the most important task we face if we want to survive and succeed overseas. In spite of this truth, maintaining healthy friendships back home is also a vital mission partnership we must consider.

Whether we obtain a regular job overseas or go with a mission agency, we will enhance our chances of success by embracing the responsibility of nurturing close friendships within our church back home. These relationships are not the normal ones we may have with church pastors and mission boards. Church staff and committees can change and may only require surface relationships. We must develop genuine friendships of trust with some individuals and families in our home church and maintain them via correspondence and phone calls. Moreover, when home for a visit, we should not wait for them to contact us, but we should be proactive and seek them out. Healthy relationships are two-way. These close relationships provide a real connection to the congregation, enhancing the partnership.

Because extensive disconnect happens after we move overseas, we need to develop healthy accountability friendships before we leave and then stay in touch at some level once there. Even if we are simply working in a job overseas, we still need prayer support, encouragement, and accountability from these friends back home. Once again, while we hope our new Christian commu-

> *It is sad when people have serious breakdowns on the field, and those back home are the last to hear about it.*

nity can help navigate the solutions, many on-field problems and challenges are often best dealt with through the prayers, encouragement, and counsel from these home church relationships.

Keeping a few key friends in our home church fully informed and up-to-date is vital for a healthy and successful experience overseas. It is sad when people have serious breakdowns on the field, and those back home are the last to hear about it. Missionary attrition often occurs because of personal burnout, marriage struggles, and family issues. While getting help from those on the field should be the first line of defense, strong friends back home can be vital in getting the help we need on the field. Having that level of trust goes a long way when struggles happen so far away.

Success in life is about good relationships. Just like any partnership in life, its success depends on strong healthy relationships of trust, both on the field and back home. Moreover, many have testified that the biggest factor in a successful re-entry back home after a time overseas was the quality of the friendships they had maintained with those in their home church and local Christian community.

Missionary Support Network

If we are considering an extended period of overseas ministry, we should develop a support network which can work in symphony to make sure all our needs are met, both at home and abroad. This network is particularly important for those working overseas without a traditional mission agency affiliation. Experience has shown that when someone takes the initiative to develop his/her own network system of support groups at home and on the field, it establishes a strong platform for healthy and effective ministry. In this chapter, we have looked at the partners we need at home, and we will consider our on-field partners in later chapters.

I. AT HOME
A. Church Advocate Group
A group of church members who rally support and prayer for us. They recognize that their church is sending us out and is ultimately responsible to make sure we are surviving and thriving on the field.

B. Practical Support Group
A group of friends who assist us with state-side practical needs like mailing, banking, furlough housing, vehicles, and other administrative responsibilities. These people are the hands and feet for our needs back home.

II. ON THE FIELD

A. Ministry Development Group

A few ministry colleagues on the field who can offer mentorship by giving guidance and counsel as we sharpen our skills and mature.

B. Personal Accountability Group

A network of trusted friends on the field (agency or nonagency) to whom we can submit our personal walks and ministries.

⤷ So what can we say about nurturing close relationships within a church back home?

We should develop friendships, not just "contacts" or "donors," and maintain these friendships with correspondence beyond the newsletter. If possible, we ought to spend extended periods of time with them. We must work to establish mutual ministering to each other. These friendships will be a key connection with the church over the long haul and will solidify a healthy relationship with that local church. They will provide a place of trust, a source of encouragement, a haven for sharing struggles, and a resource for finding the best solutions to problems. They can also rally support and assist with practical needs back home.

⤷ Jamie and Deb chose to contact some of their key friends at their home church for prayer and counsel. They needed a third party perspective on the difficulties they faced on the field. These close friends were able to give a healthy perspective and some practical wisdom in how to proceed. They decided to take an unscheduled trip to the States. During this time home, they were given some insightful books and godly counsel. While the hospital workplace clearly needed some intervention and conflict resolution, this outside help from Jamie and Deb's

friends was vital for helping them cope and thrive in a difficult situation. With this fresh perspective and renewal, Jamie and Deb felt they had the knowledge and strength to speak with the hospital leadership and propose some solutions.

Discussion Questions (Group or Mentor)

1. Why is building strong relationships of trust at your home church so important when overseas?

2. What particular role can they play when you are overseas? What about when on home visit?

3. How can these church relationships help in solving on-field issues?

4. Why is trust such an important issue when interacting with a church?

5. Why is it your responsibility to maintain these relationships?

6. If our goal is to "dig in" with locals when overseas, why do we need these outside relationships back home?

7. How do we find a healthy balance in focusing on new friendships on the field and communicating with friends back home?

Homework Assignments

Write about your present relationship with your home church. (2-3 pg) Include the following in your paper:

> The history and depth of these relationships

> Names of four or five individuals/families with whom you have a trusting relationship in your church

> Names of any leaders in the church with whom you have built a close friendship

> Any of these people listed above who are mentors whom you trust with personal struggles

> How you plan to maintain these relationships while overseas

> The names and contact information of those people who will fulfill the roles in your support network at home and on the field. (Church Advocate Group, Practical Support Group, On-Field Ministry Development Group, and Personal Accountability Group)

Chapter 8

Considering a Mission Organization

Should You Work With a Mission Agency?

"Set apart for me Barnabas and Saul
for the work to which I have called them."
Acts 13:2

~ *Mark and Jan sat on their couch with five applications and dozens of emails from different mission organizations. Their heads were spinning with all the pros and cons of each group and proposal. This kind of work was all new to them, and they were apprehensive about submitting their personal and work lives to a hierarchy of different leaders, ranging from headquarters, regional, city, and team. Every mission organization has various kinds of written covenants to sign, from agency to local team agreements. While everything on paper sounded thrilling and positive, Mark and Jan were not sure how to proceed. While their phone calls with the home offices in the U.S. were helpful and encouraging, they knew this decision had more ramifications than a normal job offer in the U.S. This partnership would launch them into a lifestyle very different from their present one. They will have a different kind of income, living in a new country with new bosses, new friends, a new culture, and a new language. While in some ways it all seemed so exciting and gave them a chance to take a great step of faith, they recognized the implications and wanted to make the wisest decision for themselves.*

People often assume that mission agencies are simply the global mission arm of the Church and the best partner for finishing the task of global discipleship. Yet much debate centers on whether mission organizations have taken too much of the local church's responsibilities while the church has forfeited its role in equipping and sending people into global missions. Many mission agencies today are working hard to establish stronger partnerships with local churches to see healthy integration between these two structures. Moreover, churches are working harder to retake their responsibilities for equipping healthy cross-cultural disciples for long-term effective cross-cultural ministry. While the debate continues, we must ask a few questions regarding the role of mission organizations.

› Whose role is it to screen, counsel, and equip healthy disciples who can be trained for cross-cultural ministry throughout the world?

› What role can a mission agency play in this process without taking on responsibilities meant for the local church?

- ➤ What key issues should we consider when deciding whether to enter a target country with a regular job at a local institution or with a traditional foreign mission agency? Can we do both?

- ➤ What are the key criteria when choosing which mission agency is the best one for the task to which God has called me and my family?

Sometimes we fail to consider why we go with a mission agency. We do not research the function, strengths, and limitations of mission organizations. We need to learn how an agency partnership can assist us in achieving success overseas as well as how such a partnership could limit our effectiveness in a particular locale. Our research should include interviewing and corresponding with those who have gone out with an agency and those who have gone without one. Is it possible for someone to acculturate successfully, maintain healthy accountability, and achieve fruitful ministry overseas without a mission organization?

It may be wise to visit the prospective field to meet with people who are with agencies as well as with those working regular jobs in-country. This way we can learn the on-field reputations and realities of working under mission agencies serving in that target area. Some agencies have a lot of experience in a particular part of the world or in a particular ministry, while others are fairly new to a region. Crucial differences can exist between home office visions and values versus actual on-the-field everyday life.

Having open communication regarding expectations of all parties (the couple, their local church leadership, and the agency leadership) prior to joining the mission organization fosters success on the field. On-field conflicts related to agency policies, decisions, and reactions to situations often stem from unclear expectations of all those involved. While many issues may be mentioned in a general orientation/training session, many candidates are learning to ask more questions and get specific about how things actually work. Such communication gives clarity for the new partnership, with each side knowing the expectations of the other. Otherwise, problems may arise later on the field when someone says, "*I just assumed that the agency would deal with this*" or "*We figured this was something the home office would not have to know about.*" We must not assume anything, but make sure we and our families have asked all the questions necessary to have clarity and peace.

Some Christians move overseas without formal mission agency affiliation and have found success in ministry. Those who follow this path can testify to having to deal with a different set of challenges. Each of us must know our own personalities and work styles. Some of us are disciplined self-starters who work well without formal structures and guidelines. On the

> *We must not assume anything...*

other hand, these kinds of people must also recognize the need for establishing relationships for fellowship, accountability, and ministry partnership. No one who heads overseas should ever think he or she can make it alone. Choosing not to affiliate with a mission agency does not mean we should isolate ourselves from or not partner with other believers in town. We would simply be choosing to use our work as a ministry platform and link up with others on the field in voluntary partnerships instead of pre-field organizational partnerships. We are all called to "*submit to one another*" (Ephesians 5:21), and God says, "*Two are better than one because they have a good return for their work*" (Ecclesiastes 4:9). Everyone who works overseas and seeks to serve the kingdom of God must walk in community within some structure, whether it be formal or informal. The task before us is to discern which arrangement is the best partnership for us in light of our personalities, work style, ministry philosophy, and particular overseas field.

Mission organizations often emphasize the value of teamwork on the field. With or without an agency, Christians are called to work in partnership for God's work. Some have found large missionary teams to be cumbersome and difficult to manage. They have chosen instead to establish their own "team" with a few co-workers on the field. Experience consistently shows that smaller teams are more efficient and easier to keep on task. Let us remember the goal is not just to find the best mission organization or simply to obtain work in a foreign land. Our goal is to find the best way for us and our family to enter a culture, master the language, get connected, and effectively engage the people for long-term impact.

ꙮ So, what have we learned about the issues involved in partnering with a mission organization?

If we choose not to partner with a mission agency, we should know what we are getting into. If we choose to partner with one, however, we should understand the function of an agency, its strengths and limitations. Before we sign with an organization, we should know what it can and cannot do for us and our ministry. It can be wise to see a mission agency at work on the field by visiting teams overseas. We must know what we are expecting from an organization and what they expect from us. Unrealistic or improper expectations can lead to serious conflicts. However, open and clear communication on the front end can establish a strong mission partnership and a powerful support structure for anyone heading overseas.

    After receiving wise counsel, Mark and Jan began to find out the on-field realities of working with a mission agency overseas. They interviewed many couples, some home for furlough and others on the field. They asked these couples direct, hard questions about the pros and cons of their agency partnerships. They arranged to take time off from work to visit two potential fields, stay with different couples from different organizations, and interview a variety of workers living in country. They were also able to interview some couples who had chosen not to partner with a mission agency. All this research gave Mark and Jan a clearer picture of the positive benefits and realistic limitations of mission agencies and field teams. Now they could better proceed in their decision process.

Discussion Questions (Group or Mentor)

1. What are the main purposes of a mission organization?

2. What are the things an agency cannot do for you?

3. Why might someone choose not to join a mission agency?

4. What are the best ways to learn about how an agency really works?

5. Do you believe someone can obtain regular employment in a country as well as develop a partnership with a mission organization overseas?

6. Do you believe going with a mission agency would bring more benefits to your mission endeavor or create more problems for your ministry? Explain what you have learned and heard.

Homework Assignments

Write out your present understanding of the purpose of mission agencies. (2-3 pg) Include the following in your paper:

➤ Wisdom gained from interviewing two or three mission agency representatives regarding the main benefits of going with a organization to your target country

➤ What you learned from an interview with two or three missionaries regarding the advantages and disadvantages of partnering with a mission agency

➤ Insights from two or three missionaries who chose not to go with an agency, their reasons for doing so and the method they used to enter the country and operate there

➤ Other counsel about choosing an organizational partnership

➤ Your own conclusions in regards to the best method for entering your target country and your reasons why

Chapter 9

Establishing A Platform
In-Country

Could a Tentmaking Job Be Strategic?

*"For though I am free from all men, I have made myself
a slave to all, that I might win the more."*
1 Corinthians 9:19

〰〰 Dave and Cindy desired to move to a country closed
to traditional mission work. He had studied petroleum
engineering, and she had a teaching degree. Both of them
had been working in their fields for the past four years. If they
moved overseas, they could operate under a made-up "cover
job" and focus totally on language and ministry outreach for
several years. Or they could pursue genuine employment with
a company or school within the country. While their purpose
for going was clearly gospel outreach, they did not know why

they had to drop their careers to engage in overseas ministry. Moreover, they did not have peace about entering a new culture without a clear identity. Their dialogue with several mission organizations had resulted in some frustration. The particular agencies were not interested in their vocational backgrounds. Moreover, the agencies would not allow them to work with jobs in-country for the first three years. While Dave and Cindy felt strongly about having legitimate work platforms, the mission groups were concerned with how this work would affect their language learning.

T he typical path of entering overseas ministry today is to partner with a mission organization. Much can be gained from an agency's experience, on-ground connections, and staff support. In addition to this organizational and missionary team partnership, many fields require Christian workers to have some sort of vocational platform in-country. The goal is to create an association within the local society. This local partnership can establish residency, local credibility, and natural relationships. While in theory the idea of wearing two hats looks good, the reality is that many find it difficult to balance these two commitments. On the one hand, they are trying to justify the financial support they receive by focusing on ministry opportunities, and on the other hand, they are attempting to fulfill the responsibilities of the job platform. They find themselves torn between achieving ministry goals and sustaining a business or teaching job. They realize that if they are successful in running a platform business but never gain language fluency, they will be ineffective in ministry impact. While some have found a healthy balance, many live in a constant struggle. Some end up severing one of the partnerships in order to focus on the other. Either they focus on ministry and simply maintain the appearance of a job by carrying a business card and operating an office, or they decide to have no mission agency tie and focus on doing a regular business, letting ministry flow from their engagement in society.

The point we want to stress here is that whether we enter with or without a mission agency partnership, it is very important to establish natural associations with the target group. In fact, instead of focusing on their choice of mission agency association, many are finding the value of obtaining jobs in the target country as a way of partnership. They make a local, in-country establishment their platform base for relationships and ministry opportunities. Sometimes we can rely on the missionary community for identity rather than bonding with locals. Some have found success in simply working at a local school or company while still maintaining fellowship and accountability by linking up with other ex-pats in town. This model puts a higher emphasis on establishing a bona fide presence in society and bonding with the local people and less focus on the foreign agency and team partnerships. It works particularly well in pioneer fields where traditional mission work is extremely limited.

Sometimes we can rely on the missionary community for identity rather than bonding with locals.

Some have left the field prematurely because they got worn down by the identity crisis created by having no legitimate presence in the community. Others have left because they failed to enter society and build normal friendships from which to establish genuine witness. Those who view themselves primarily as "foreign missionaries" or "church-planters" may struggle with finding an identity and connecting in society. But if they see themselves as teachers, businessmen or consultants who are there to live missionally, incorporating the gospel into their whole life throughout the day, they may find it easier to enter and engage with the target society. Even international companies operating overseas have learned that establishing the right local associations within a target country is vital to entering and operating successfully in a new cross-cultural environment.

When training missionary candidates, we may put too much emphasis on "establishing contacts" and "planting churches" and fail to give them legitimate ways *into* the society and pathways that create *doors* into people's lives. We give them a lot of information about the message and about facilitating church gatherings. If, however, we do not show them how to actually *connect and partner* with people in this new society, the gospel fails to penetrate.

We may put too much emphasis on "establishing contacts" and "planting churches" and fail to give them legitimate ways into the society

Regardless of how we enter a country and our organizational affiliation, establishing a platform can assist us in connecting and engaging with society. The goal is once again to use the platform to enter the culture, gain language fluency, and make an impact in people's lives.

↪ So what can we say about the value of establishing a platform in the new society?

Many have been successful in maintaining a healthy relationship with both a foreign missionary team and the local society. Others have found great success in entering a country with a local institution or company as the main partnership, while still establishing healthy accountability and fellowship within the local Christian community. Whichever path we choose, we must find legitimate ways to connect with the new society.

We need to do our homework, therefore, to find out the best method to enter the particular society we are targeting. Choosing the right target society platform is one of the vital mission partner decisions we have to make. Taking short exploratory trips into target countries can aid us in discovering platform opportunities that are available.

After much dialogue and negotiating with one particular mission organization, Dave and Cindy were able to find an agreeable solution which satisfied both groups' goals. While agreeing to partner with a mission agency, the couple would seek out a job agreement with a company and/ or institution in-country. This arrangement would allow them to complete a full-time language course before beginning employment. They would grasp a foundation in the language for the first four months and then continue in language study in a part-time fashion. This plan gave Dave and Cindy a solid platform for identity and natural ministry, while also giving them the mission partnership they wanted.

Discussion Questions (Group or Mentor)

1. Do you know any missionaries who have chosen simply to enter a country with a job at a local institution/company (tentmakers)?

2. What are the key benefits in using this method of partnership?

3. Why would having a platform affect the way locals interact with you?

4. What are the inherent dangers in this way of working in a foreign land?

5. How would you caution someone who is considering this method?

6. Is it possible to have a genuine tentmaking job overseas and also be able to do cross-cultural evangelism/discipleship/church planting?

7. What are your thoughts on full-time ministry vs. a marketplace job?

Homework Assignments:

Write out your present understanding and conclusions regarding the value of platform jobs overseas. (3-5 pg) *Include the following in your paper:*

> The most important benefits of making a foreign institution a key partnership in entering/working in a country

> Lessons from three missionaries who went with traditional mission agencies regarding having a job platform in-country (tentmaking)

> Five warnings and five suggestions from three missionaries who held regular jobs in-country overseas

> Your own conclusions about establishing a job platform in your target country

> Insights gained from interviews with mission agency representatives about organizational policies regarding in-country jobs

Chapter 10

Determining On-Field Team Expectations

How Well Do You Know Your Team?

"So then we pursue the things which make
for peace and the building up of one another."
Romans 14:19

⁓ *Paul and Diane had been on the mission field for one year, working within a traditional missionary team in a large city. They had first met their teammates at an orientation week in the U.S. and had gotten to know them more via Internet calls and emails. The first seven months had been very encouraging, and they had found needed support from their fellow teammates. The past several months, however, had brought discouragement and stress. It began with a few misunderstandings from poor communication, but recently the conflicts had increased. Some issues seemed petty, but other issues reflected clear differences in values and philosophy among teammates. The team leader had made several attempts to bring unity and understanding. It seemed, however, that the strong differences had brought everyone to an impasse. In spite of all the stresses of adjusting to a new culture and language, Paul and Jan found that the main source of anxiety was their missionary team.*

Many find great communion in spirit, fellowship in love and cooperation in ministry by being a part of a missionary team during their time overseas. Yet others say the stress created by team expectations and inter-personal conflicts was the greatest source of heartaches and became an actual hindrance to a fruitful experience overseas. Just as in entering any other kind of partnership, anyone planning to join a traditional pre-field missionary team should proceed wisely. They should know the kinds of questions to ask everyone involved prior to joining. Once again, open communication is key.

A typical missionary team usually functions with a combination of singles and families and a team leader. Prior to joining a mission team, gaining experience working on a team in school, church or a company can provide invaluable insights. Operating on a team of different people in a foreign country can be stressful. A couple definitely needs to choose wisely the leadership to which they submit themselves and their family. How well do they know their future team leader's and teammates' expectations for them? They should find out the expectations for team meetings, friendships, Sunday worship, ministry cooperation, and children interaction. We each have our own thoughts on standards of living, holidays, entertainment, and alcohol. A key to success in working within an on-field team structure is open dialogue regarding expectations. While most enter team covenants excited and hopeful in the new partnerships, they can be naïve about the different dynamics and potential conflicts. Discussing personal boundaries and core values prior to joining a team helps ensure on-field harmony.

Some teams operate in a way where everyone is working within their different giftings, moving in different spheres of ministry but with the same ultimate goal. In this structure, members may have different ministry focuses, venues, and target groups, e.g., John is a teacher, focusing on college students; Mary works with children at a local church; Peter and Caleb run an import/export business and build relationships with the business community. Other teams operate in a structure where everyone is using their particular giftings and jobs to work in unity for a common ministry goal. In this structure, each member uses his/her gifts for a common ministry focus, venue, and target group, e.g., all focus on evangelism/discipleship among a particular sub-group in society or neighborhood with the goal of planting a church. One of these structures could be restrictive for one type of family yet perfect for another. Each person needs to know and understand his or her approach to teamwork and ministry.

A key to success in working within an on-field team structure is open dialogue regarding expectations.

Many missionaries have found that they really needed and appreciated all the attention and support from their team in the early months of adjustment in-country. Then as time passed and they got more settled and connected with locals in town, the long weekly meetings and the constant team expectations became a burden. They ask, "*If our goal is to bond with the local people, immerse ourselves in the new culture, and master the local language, then why is there so much pressure and time spent on mission team gatherings and relationships?"* Focusing too much on teamwork development can in fact distract us from reaching out to the local people. Missiologists have said, therefore, that bonding with locals in the early months can be vital to language acquisition.

> *The newcomer who is immediately immersed in the local community has many advantages. If he lives with a local family, he can learn how the insiders organize their lives, how they get their food and do their shopping, and how they get around with public transportation. During the first couple of months, he can learn much about the insiders' attitudes and how they feel about the ways typical foreigners live. As he experiences an alternative lifestyle, he can evaluate the value of adopting it for himself and his own family. On the other hand, the missionary whose first priority is to get settled can only settle in his familiar Western way and once this is done he is virtually locked into a pattern that is foreign to the local people.*[1]

Interestingly, some couples have shared that they wish they could have had more team involvement and community building activities after their arrival overseas. Bottom line, we need to know ourselves and our own needs and limitations. We might also find it helpful to obtain some kind of teamwork experience or take a work style personality test to help us decide on the kind of work/ministry environment that fits us best.

Many have said they wish that prior to leaving they could have had candid, pre-field talks with their teammates and leaders on subjects such as conflict resolution, commitment to language study, platform jobs, approaches to accountability, controversial doctrinal issues, worship styles, church government, conversion/baptism issues, philosophy of child-rearing, choice of entertainment, alcohol usage, leadership styles, friendships outside the team, and even clothing styles. Sadly, team conflicts can cause the main stresses on the field, as opposed to conflicts with the local peoples or authorities. A good team relationship can be a blessing overseas, but a bad team relationship can be a huge burden.

> *Sadly, team conflicts can cause the main stresses on the field.*

Author Patrick Lencioni believes the typical dysfunctions of a team can be avoided by means of open communication. In his book *The Five Dysfunctions of a Team,* Lencioni writes:

> *Team members who are not genuinely open with each other about their mistakes and weaknesses make it impossible to build a foundation of trust. Teams that lack trust are incapable of engaging in unfiltered and passionate debate of ideas. Instead, they resort to veiled discussions and guarded comments.*[2]

He says this deficiency in trust and honesty on a team leads to a lack of commitment, an avoidance of accountability and eventually inattention to results. This chain of dysfunctions begins with the absence of open, honest dialogue. We cannot begin this trust building communication after a team has been put together, but it must begin before we submit ourselves and family to a team that will operate thousands of miles away overseas.

In addition to the normal differences that exist between individuals with different personalities, backgrounds, and regions in the U.S., culture expert David Livermore says in his book, *Cultural Intelligence: Improving Your CQ to Engage*

Our Multicultural World, fifty percent of today's overseas missionaries originate from places other than North America and Western Europe. So those missionaries working overseas must not only work to understand the cultural dynamics of working in a particular country but also grasp the dynamics of working with teammates and co-workers from various cultures.[3] Moreover, Livermore says there are three main cross-cultural contexts in our lives: socio-ethnic, organizational, and generational. We must be prepared to deal with one or all of these on a missionary team.[4]

ᔐ So what can we say about on-field missionary team expectations?

Before we join a team, we need to know many things about our future teammates and leaders. We should learn about their expectations, values in regards to team life, ministry goals, and a host of other topics. We should learn how the team is expected to function and if there is a limit on the size of the team. A small committed few can be very effective. If our relationship with the team leader and teammates is not healthy, our line of accountability on the field can be broken, leaving us vulnerable to numerous problems. We need to be honest and not rush into a decision. We may need to slow down the process and create ways to find out more about our team. We all know the wisdom in dating someone before rushing into marriage! Ultimately, good partnerships on the field are those that empower us to remain healthy, stay on task, and make an impact.

A small committed few can be very effective.

ᔐ *Unfortunately, Paul and Diane's team ended up breaking apart, and several of them returned to the States. They themselves decided to stay on in the country and begin the process of joining another group. But this time, they decided to proceed more slowly and get to know their future teammates better. Together as a couple Paul and Diane prepared a list of important issues they felt needed to be discussed with their potential teammates. They sought out informal times to talk about a variety of issues with each team member. Moreover, they took opportunities to spend time together, doing both fun activities and ministry. This time they wanted more information and clarity before entering into a team commitment relationship.*

Discussion Questions (Group or Mentor)

1. What would be the benefits of working on a team in a foreign country?

2. What do you believe would be the potential problems involved in working on a pre-field assembled mission team?

3. Could you suggest a good way to assemble a mission team?

4. In light of the many differences in beliefs, values, personalities, giftings, and working styles, what do you believe is necessary for teammates to do prior to departure in order to have a successful team experience?

5. Where do you believe the most common conflicts arise on a team?

6. Do you believe it is possible to not go with a formal team structure and yet seek out relationships within the community for informal partnerships, Christian fellowship, and personal accountability?

7. What would you think of someone arriving on the field, getting established in language/culture, and then developing a team there?

Homework Assignments

1. Write out your present understanding of your on-field team expectations. (2-3 pg) Include the following in your paper:

> ‣ Advice from three missionaries regarding the greatest benefits of being on a missionary team while living and serving overseas

> ‣ Honest thoughts from these three missionaries regarding what they saw as the main sources of team conflict and how they were resolved

> ‣ Input regarding a team's "memo of understanding" or "team covenant"

> ‣ Key findings from researching three mission organizations regarding team formation, on-field team functions, and various leadership styles

> ‣ What you have learned about mission teams and expectations, your conclusions on this subject and how you want to proceed with a team

2. Take the DiSC® *Workplace Test* to understand your work style better and to appreciate the style of how others work.

Chapter 10 Notes

1 E. Thomas Brewster and Elizabeth S. Brewster, "The Difference Bonding Makes" in *Perspectives on the World Christian Movement: a Reader* (3rd Edition], Ralph D Winter et al., (Pasadena: William Carey Library, 1999), 445.

2 Patrick Lencioni, *The Five Dysfunctions of a Team: A Leadership Fable* (San Francisco: Jossey-Bass, 2002), 188.

3 David A Livermore, *Cultural Intelligence: Improving Your CQ to Engage Our Multicultural World* (Grand Rapids: Baker Academic, 2009), 28.

4 Ibid., 15.

Part II Action List
The PARTNERS

☐ **6. Seriously Consider Your Family Needs**

Make sure your most valuable partners, your spouse and children, are on board, feel protected, and understand the expectations upon them for this overseas cross-cultural endeavor.

☐ **7. Establish Home Church Friendships**

Cultivate some genuine friendships of trust within your home church and community to be sources of encouragement, support, and wisdom to you both on the field and when home.

☐ **8. Research Mission Organizations**

Learn the advantages of mission agencies, discover the important criteria to consider when choosing one, and research different agencies, including their on-field reputations and realities.

☐ **9. Consider a Platform Job In-Country**

Research ways in which you can establish a partnership or employment under a local institution or company in the target country and learn from those who have attempted to establish such partnerships overseas.

☐ **10. Know On-Field Team Expectations**

Take sufficient time to get to know your team, their expectations and discuss openly key topics such as doctrine, church, children, leadership styles, philosophy of ministry, team size, and conflict resolution.

Part II Further Reading
The PARTNERS

Ask a Missionary Time-tested Answers from Those Who've Been There Before. John McVay, Gen. Ed. Downers Grove, IL: Inter-Varsity Press, 2010.

Boundaries: When to Say Yes, How to Say No to Take Control of Your Life. Henry Cloud and John Sims Townsend. Grand Rapids, MI: Zondervan Pub. House, 1992.

Friend Raising: Building a Missionary Support Team That Lasts. Betty J. Barnett. Seattle, WA: YWAM Pub., 2003.

Today's Tentmakers: Self-support-an Alternative Model for Worldwide Witness. J. Christy Wilson. Eugene, OR: Wipf and Stock Publishers, 2002.

Business as Mission: A Comprehensive Guide to Theory and Practice Common. C. Neal Johnson. Downers Grove, IL: Inter-Varsity Press, 2010.

The Missional Entrepreneur: Principles and Practices for Business as Mission. Mark Russell. Birmingham, AL: New Hope Publishers, 2010.

The Five Dysfunctions of a Team: a Leadership Fable. Patrick Lencioni. San Francisco, CA: Jossey-Bass, 2002.

Part III

The PLACE

*A vital part of astronaut training at NASA
is basic training in how to survive and thrive
in the new environment while
successfully accomplishing the mission.*

*What are the critical questions we need to consider in
order to survive, thrive, and do effective cross-cultural
ministry in the PLACE we hope to serve?*

Chapter 11

Assessing the People Group

Do You Know Your Target People?

Paul, standing in the midst of the Areopagus, said:
"Men of Athens, I perceive that in every way
you are very religious."
Acts 17:22

     ~   *Chris was interested in reaching Arabs with the gospel. The only information he had was from books, prayer guides, and one Arab friend from college. He contacted organizations working in the Middle East and began the interview process. He had visited one Arab people group on a short-term mission trip but was not sure that was the country in which he wanted to serve. Once he had decided which agency to join, he went to see his church missions pastor. The pastor asked Chris about his experience with Arabic peoples and countries. During the discussion, Chris learned that there were many Arabs living right in his own city, and the pastor suggested some ways for meeting them. The pastor counseled Chris to work at narrowing down which Arab people he would target in order to bring focus to his research and vision.*

Westerners are notoriously famous for global ignorance. We make gross generalizations and foster stereotypes regarding the ethnic and language groups in the world. How easy it is for us to label peoples of the world into groups like "Europeans," "Asians," "Middle Easterners" and "Africans," ignoring the mosaic of thousands of distinct ethnic groups that live in regions that encompass three to four geopolitical countries. We hear people say, "*I want to work among Indians,*" when there are in fact two thousand different ethnic groups living in India. When we speak of "Iranians," we should remember there are Persians, Assyrians, Jews, Turkmen, Azeri, Kurds, Baluch, and Arabs within the borders of Iran.

> *Stemming from gross naïveté or pride, we assume the reason the gospel has not taken root among a people group is simply that the message has not been preached to them.*

We must be careful when we set out to bring solutions to problems created over thousands of years of culture, religion, and politics. Each people group in the world has its own unique history, culture, and religious context. Stemming from gross naïveté or pride, we assume the reason the gospel has not taken root among a people group is simply that the message has not been preached to them. We underestimate the centuries of bad history and the layers of social, religious, and cultural complexities that create prejudices and misunderstandings of the message being presented. Long before the message of the Cross has a chance to affront the listener, the target people can be offended by the cultural trappings associated with the gospel or the particular foreigner bringing the message. The task of contextualizing the pure gospel message for a people group involves attempting to live out and speak of the message of Christ in such a way that the listeners do not falsely believe they must completely reject their own culture and embrace a new foreign culture in order to follow Christ.

If we are hoping to move overseas to take the gospel into a foreign culture, our first task is to assess the history and current state of the gospel within a particular people group. Online articles, books, and interviews can inform us about the

Unreached people are living right in your own city

people, their culture, their church history, the present political situation, and the present needs of the people. Then we must pro-actively research and discover whether we have the particular talents, skills, and giftings that can help the people group we are hoping to reach. We cannot completely leave this decision to a church or agency.

We should visit the country and interview missionaries and local leaders to find out the actual needs in the country and in the particular people groups there. We should research the greatest hindrances to the gospel in this place. This research must also involve understanding the differences between urban and rural, traditional and modern, rich and poor, majority and minority, orthodox and animistic. We need to know the present atmosphere towards Christianity and the political climate towards the West. We should find out how they view foreigners coming into their land. It would be helpful to know foreigners who have entered and made effective contributions there. Before we choose a country, an agency or our own strategy, we need to listen to both nationals and experienced workers to hear the best ways to assist the local believers to reach their own people with the gospel. Then we must ask ourselves if these kinds of ministries fit with our own giftings.

Researching ways to engage with the people group right in our own hometown or nearby city constitutes another part of the assessment process. Is it not interesting that often people who believe they are called to a people group in a far away land have never found out if any of these unreached people are living right in their own city? We can learn much about a particular people group by engaging with some of these people who have come to our country as well as by interviewing people who have been working with them here in our country.

Short Exploration Trips

Any sort of travel overseas exposes us to other cultures and can give us a feel for cross-cultural living conditions, lifestyles, and language. A one- to two-week prepared outreach or work project mission trip overseas is limited, however, in showing us what real life and ministry is like overseas. For exposure and vision for overseas ministry, a better option might be to take a smaller group (3-5 people) with a focused purpose of "exploring the land." The participants would investigate the needs of a country, interact with veteran workers, spend time with families working there, and research creative-access jobs and ministry opportunities for future long-term work. At first glance, this kind of trip may appear

...get a much clearer picture of the task as they observe families doing overseas ministry in real cross-cultural environments.

to be focused on the "goers" instead of impacting the target group. More thoughtful observation reveals, however, that participants can get a much clearer picture of the task and learn how they may fit, as they observe and learn from families doing overseas ministry in real cross-cultural environments. They will see workers seeking to juggle the tasks of learning a language, developing relationships, and raising a family. The research gained regarding the actual needs, ministry opportunities, and possible job platforms would be invaluable to young people trying to decide on a college major and discover their place in God's mission to the nations.

So, what can we say about assessing a country and people group?

We must pray and research to narrow down our target people group. If our goal is to make a positive impact upon this group of people, it would be wise to interview others to discover what has been attempted, what has worked, and what has not. We need to assess the types of ministries these people actually need and the opportunities open to foreigners. What are the best ways to empower the locals there to reach their own people? While the specifics of what we will be able to do must be worked out after we have been in the country for some time and learned the language and culture, before we leave, we should learn as much as possible about the state of the church in that land, the existing needs, and the open doors for our particular giftings and expertise. The best plan may be, in fact, to not move to a place but seek to empower the locals there in their own ministries through small business development and bible training.

After spending several months getting to know people from the country in which he was interested, Chris learned many new things about these people. He participated in some of their cultural activities, experienced their hospitality, and discovered some of their attitudes, misunderstandings, and beliefs regarding the gospel. As Chris interacted with different families in town, he began to develop a personal strategy for how he might work among these people. He even learned about a vocational skill which he could use to enter their country and serve them.

Suggested Resources

> *Operation World* (www.operationworld.org)

> *Perspectives on the World Christian Movement* (www.perspectives.org)

> *Pathways To Global Understanding* (www.pathways2.org)

> *Prayer Cast* (www.prayercast.org)

> *Joshua Project* (www.joshuaproject.net)

Discussion Questions (Group or Mentor)

1. Why do you think Christians remain content with viewing the unreached as "over there" and do not take steps to engage them right here?

2. Why is researching a country's church history and present needs so important when trying to decide where you can serve?

3. How can knowing a people's actual needs as well as your spiritual strengths work together in your mission journey?

4. Why do you think Westerners are culturally ignorant and can over-simplify the task of reaching a people group?

5. Discuss ways in which western Christians can actually hinder healthy church growth by not entering with a humble spirit that seeks to listen and understand the culture and real needs.

Homework Assignments

Write out your plan to research and discover the state of the gospel among a people group and an entry strategy to help the church there. (3-5 pg) Include the following in your paper:

> Lessons from three missionaries about ways to gain understanding of the present needs of a people group

> Insights from three national Christians (living here or in their own countries) on how a foreigner can best enter, learn, serve, and empower locals to reach their own people with the gospel

> Your next steps for researching the country and people group and learning their church history, religious prejudices, cultural barriers, nationalistic attitudes, and political climate

> How you met three to five people from your target people here in your home city and built friendships with them

> Insights from these friends regarding the challenges for the gospel among that group

Chapter 12

Connecting and Belonging in Society

What Will Be Your Identity?

*"Jesus kept increasing in wisdom and stature,
and in favor with God and men."*
Luke 2:52

〜 *Jason had met many people from a particular people group who were living right in his own city in the U.S. He was enjoying his friendships with several of them. He decided it would be wise to make a visit to their homeland and learn more about how he might reach them with the gospel. One family suggested he stay with their relatives in a particular city during his visit. Jason made arrangements to visit Christian workers in the country as well as stay with his new friends' relatives. While on this trip, Jason researched some of the felt needs there and ways in which foreigners have obtained residence and work. The foreigners living there mentioned how suspicious the local people were about Westerners living among them. He discovered that if he wanted to find a way to get connected there, he would need to rethink his entry plan.*

While we and our supporting churches know who we are and why we are living in a foreign country, the people in the new country have no idea who we are, why we have come and whether we are there for their good or harm. While we desire to bring good news to them, the history, media, and culture of the people may be telling them foreigners bring mostly bad things. If we as outsiders hope to influence people, our first task is to get connected. *"No task is more important in the first years of ministry in a new culture than the building of trusting relationships with the people."*[1] Therefore, we must figure out a way to enter this new society, connect with the community, find appropriate ways to be culturally accepted and "belong" within that society so we can build authentic relationships.

If we as outsiders hope to influence people, our first task is to get connected.

When we arrive into the new culture, it is normal in the early months to link up with the English-speaking expatriate community, but over time this attachment can hinder our ability to bond with the local people. While these ex-pat relationships are vital for fellowship and accountability, we cannot overemphasize the importance of working hard in the early years to build bonding relationships with the people. To build this connection, we have to find a way to "belong" in the new environment. Local residents must feel good about our presence in their community if we ever want to build trust with them. Duane Elmer in his invaluable book *Cross-Cultural Servanthood* says, "*The most important step in entering a new culture is to build trust. Only when people trust us will they listen to what we have to say.*"[2] When trust is established, real learning begins. These friends with whom we have built trust become our teachers, insiders, and bridges in the new culture. As mentioned earlier, having a legitimate reason for being there (genuine work/service) is a natural avenue for belonging in society and connecting with people. These platforms enable us to serve the local community and build authentic relationships. It is in these relationships that we learn what the people do, why they do it and the underlying values of their behavior and culture.

Westerners are generally independent people who value doing everything for themselves, but we must break this habit by expressing to locals that we need help from them to live, survive, and understand their way of life. When we probe their thoughts with questions and seek understanding, we are saying, in

> *Platforms enable us to serve the local community and build authentic relationships.*

effect, "*I need you to teach me, I cannot do this alone, and I do not have all the answers!*"

Instead of trying to find spiritual "seekers" or "contacts," newcomers should commit themselves to spending lots of time with a variety of local people. Sometimes our theological and evangelistic training keep us from pursuing anyone the Lord puts in our path. The early years are about observing and learning the language and culture, not about ministry strategy. We arrive disconnected to the people, and we must take as many opportunities as we can to dive in and get connected. We ask the Lord to guide us every day and then get out there and start meeting people. If we get an invitation to someone's home, we accept it and "*eat what is set before [us]*" (Luke

10:8). If we meet someone at work or school, we pursue ways of engaging them on their turf. Some of these new friends can become key relationships for getting connected and belonging in the new place.

⌾ So what can we say about the value of connecting and belonging in a society as part of working to be effective?

Finding a way to connect and belong opens doors for bonding and building relationships of trust. These friendships foster genuine learning and authentic partnerships that can replace the "Us-Them" mindset with a "We" mindset in ministry.[3] Then we can begin to work together to discover the best ways for the target people to reach their own with the gospel through culturally sensitive means, bringing lasting fruit. Moreover, these close relationships with locals are vital for someone acculturating and thriving in the new environment. If we do not engage with locals at this deep level, we remain disconnected. Nothing is more miserable than living in strange surroundings year after year and always feeling foreign. We must get connected and find a way to belong there.

⌁ *Jason's short trip to his target country proved invaluable in discovering the task before him. He was able to see some Christian workers who seemed connected in society and others who lacked connections. He appreciated how one ex-pat had used his giftings in sports to enter a coaching job, which launched his family into many natural relationships in the community. Jason began to think more about his own giftings and vocational skills, and how he might use them in gaining an entry point into the society.*

Discussion Questions (Group or Mentor)

1. Some foreigners who have come to your city have connected in their communities and found ways to contribute and belong in society, and others have not. What can you observe about the differences?

2. What are the key factors which contribute to these newcomers' getting connected and finding a way to "belong" here?

3. How do you feel about those who do not connect? Do you trust them?

4. Why do you believe finding this "connecting point" is key to building relationships of trust?

5. Westerners tend to be more individualistic and independent than other cultures. How do you believe this can hinder getting connected?

Homework Assignments

Write out what you have learned about getting connected and belonging in a society. (3-5 pg) Include the following in your paper:

> Lessons from three immigrants (Christian or non-Christian) who have been in your city for several years about:
  * what helped them connect and what hindered them
  * what has contributed to their feeling that they belong
  * ways they have found to contribute to their neighbor and community

> Insights from three people who have lived overseas about
  * what helped them get connected to society
  * what contributed to their sense of belonging

> Your own strategy for entering the target society and getting connected and belonging there

Chapter 12 Notes

1   Paul G. Hiebert, *Anthropological Insights for Missionaries* (Grand Rapids: Baker Book House, 1985), 85.

2   Duane Elmer, *Cross-cultural Servanthood: Serving the World in Christlike Humility* (Downers Grove: IVP Books, 2006), 76.

3   Ibid., 106.

Chapter 13

Learning the Language and Culture

Do You Understand Your First Task?

"And when they heard that he was addressing
them in the Hebrew language,
they became even more quiet."
Acts 22:2

~~~' *John and Kate, with their two small children, had moved overseas two years ago. Their language fluency was not progressing as well as they had hoped. They figured that after four to six months in language study, they would be functioning well and able to engage in outreach. John was struggling to find available language helpers and friends to help him. He was also a bit of an introvert and found it hard to strike up conversations in the marketplace. Responsibilities with the children kept Kate in the home a lot, and she too had*

not developed any close friends to help with language. They were becoming a bit discouraged in their language learning and even found themselves hanging out with more ex-pats than locals. Since their arrival, John and Kate had been attending an English-speaking church for fellowship and networking. Recently they were asked to be a part of the ministry team at the church to help with the worship and children. They were not sure how to proceed.

Today we observe a trend towards sending out people whose training reflects an emphasis on theology, evangelism methods, and church planting techniques. Yet the top priority in the early years must be on language and culture learning. In the past, missionaries arrived with a long-term perspective, believing they were there for a career, and understood they could do little until they learned the language, culture, and worldview of the people. Mission agencies rigorously mandated language learning *before* any ministry opportunities were considered. Some agencies even said continuation on the field was dependent on language testing scores. Today, workers often feel pressure from within themselves or from their churches to *do* something in ministry. Such expectations may stem from the focus of their Bible and missions training, from the pace of their lives before they arrived or from Western success standards.

Workers often feel pressure from within themselves to do something in ministry.

Language, Culture and Worldview

Those who have not been involved in cross-cultural ministry find it difficult to grasp the significance of language as the door to understanding a people and to effectiveness for ministry in that culture. Pioneer fields differ significantly from those fields with established national churches, Bible schools, and other Christian institutions. The latter ministries provide immediate opportunities for workers to get plugged in, link up with local ministries, attend language programs, and gain encouragement as part of the whole national movement. Coming to a field where there are few real "beach-heads" for ministry, however, can be daunting. Not everyone is a self-starter and can wait patiently for years as they learn the language and do grass-roots relationship building. During the early years, missionaries are trying to fill their prayer letters with encouraging stories of outreach and "serendipity moments." Instead, they should recognize that focusing on learning the language and culture well is, in fact, the best and most productive ministry they can do for the target people in those early years.

Language mastery is the doorway to effective, lasting impact. If someone does not learn the new language well, all the theology and church planting training remains inaccessible to the target people. Training someone in how to design buildings before they grasp the mathematics needed to make calculations is useless. While we must train candidates in what they will do when they have new followers

> *Focusing on learning the language and culture well is, in fact, the best and most productive ministry they can do.*

of Jesus, the initial focus should be on getting themselves to a place where they can be used in that context.

Unless newcomers make radical changes to their lifestyles and treat language-learning as the top priority, they may never achieve the fluency needed to be effective in cross-cultural ministry. They must spend the time and funds necessary and prepare themselves emotionally and mentally to persevere for several years. Realistic expectations for ministry are important for them, their church, and their agency in the first years. Some naïvely believe they can jump into ministry simply after becoming "functional" in the new language. Knowing the culture and worldview of a people is vital for ministry effectiveness. The language is the gateway to understanding a culture, which reveals the underlying worldview of a people.

Some mission agencies have a policy that their missionaries cannot take on a market job during their language-learning period. While focusing on language with a full-time course in the first several months is wise, many have found that working in a job has aided their language fluency. A job in town can get us out of the house, connect us in the community, and force us to use our language skills. Even an English teaching job surrounds us with locals and enhances natural opportunities to use the language. While language-learning is our "full-time job" for the first years in country, simply studying and attempting to practice the language every day for several years can be difficult for those used to a working schedule and environment. The key is to commit ourselves to using *every* task and *every* interaction as an opportunity to learn and practice the language.

Some naïvely believe they can jump into ministry simply after becoming "functional" in the new language.

When we arrive in a new land, the new culture may seem to have many holes in it, and we assume the people must be longing to fill these holes with something. But we must remember this culture has developed for hundreds, perhaps thousands of years, and has found answers to its problems, right or wrong. We must realize that this culture is not designed to make us comfortable. It is designed to make its own people comfortable. It answers their needs and wants. Understanding this is crucial.

Like Christ, we must become incarnational learners in the new culture. Cultural anthropologist Paul Hiebert says, *"Just as the infinite Creator became incarnate as a human to reach finite people, so the divine revelation must take flesh in human languages and cultures."*[1]

We lay aside the economic and social advantages of being members of a more powerful language community and, against all odds, learn the new language and take on the culture of the disadvantaged for no economic or social gain. We attempt to behold God and his Word through another lens. We humble ourselves to become like a stammering child in order to serve another and reveal the glory of the gospel. We take on the role of a listener and learner, not someone with all the answers. This task can be difficult for some because an adult is *"reluctant to act in 'childish ways.'"*[2] His self-image has been established and restrains him from behavior which he interprets as childish. He doesn't want to make childish mistakes. But to be an effective language learner, the adult must be willing to be *"child-like."*[3]

> *The culture is not designed to make us comfortable. It is designed to make its own people comfortable.*

Why do we work hard to learn a language and culture well? Because our task is to see the gospel translated into the language and culture of a people. Language acquisition expert Thomas Brewster writes,

> *"God chose translation as the mode of action for the salvation of humanity. Christian faith rests on a divine act of translation: 'the Word became flesh, and dwelt among us' (John 1:14). Any confidence we have in the translatability of the Bible rests on that prior act of translation."*[4]

We learn a language well so that we can understand another's culture as well as we know our own. We work hard at learning a language so that we can communicate meaningfully our thoughts and hearts, and hopefully exchange ideas and worldviews with another. We strive for mastery so that we can discern properly who is actually seeking spiritual things and who is not. When missionaries fill their newsletters with high numbers of professions of faith occurring on the field, but then later discover these conversions were not genuine, they can simply say *"this happens"* and *"it's hard to tell."* The problem may lie, however, in failure of these missionaries to have a good mastery of the language and deep understanding of the worldview of the people. Many mistakes on the field stem from cultural ignorance and western naïveté.

Many mistakes on the field stem from cultural ignorance and western naïveté.

Setting Our Top Priority

When entering a new culture to prepare ourselves for effective impact, it is extremely important to be clear on our top priorities.

> Is language learning priority number one?

> Are we committed to spending hundreds and hundreds of hours studying and practicing the new language?

> Is the plan to become simply functional in a language and then engaging in ministry?

> Is jumping into ministry using English even an option?

It takes perseverance for several years to gain the fluency needed for effective cross-cultural ministry. The amount of time spent with the people in real life contexts and developing genuine friendships with them can determine who learns a language well and who does not. Instead of being independent Westerners, we must learn to ask locals for help in our problems, getting things fixed, and finding things in town. Moreover, many important lifestyle choices affect our ability to focus on language and culture learning:

> ‣ Choosing the part of town and kind of community we live in

> ‣ Allocating sufficient funds for language school, tutors, and child-care

> ‣ Limiting access to English entertainment at home and office

> ‣ Deciding how often to communicate with people back home

> ‣ Putting boundaries on Internet, email, news, and social media usage

> ‣ Spending limited time with expatriates and fellow missionaries for specific periods

> ‣ Having a regular job platform in a local company or school

> ‣ Getting involved in community activities, hobbies, clubs

We may wonder how long it can take us to become proficient in a foreign language. It is impossible to answer this question because much depends on a person's language learning ability, age, motivation, learning environment, and intensity of instruction. It also depends on the level of proficiency the person wishes to attain.[5] Westerners are sometimes unaware that one of the other key factors in determining the length of time it takes to achieve proficiency is the difficulty of the language. Some languages are closely related to English while others have sig-

Lifestyle choices affect our ability to focus on language and culture learning.

nificant linguistic and cultural differences from English. We may incorrectly assume that since we did well in Spanish classes in high school, we know what is involved in studying Arabic. In general, Westerners do well in languages like Spanish, French, Italian, and German. Those, however, who have attempted to achieve fluency in languages like Turkish, Farsi, Arabic, Russian, Japanese or Chinese have found it far more difficult than they expected. The good news is that many Westerners have succeeded in learning these difficult languages through perseverance, discipline, lifestyle adjustments, and an unwavering commitment to attain fluency before anything else.

Many who go overseas to minister cross-culturally can focus too much on *what* they are going to do in ministry instead of the *how* they are going to become potentially useful. They may emphasize having a strong team and sound church planting techniques, but forget that knowing the target language well is *the* door to understanding and impacting the cultural worldviews of the people. Unless we enter through this door, our ministry can be ineffective. We can also underestimate the cost, time, and commitment required to make language study and practice the highest priority in our weekly schedules during the early years in-country.

> *Knowing the target language well is the door to understanding and impacting the cultural worldviews of the people.*

It should be stated clearly at this point that our ministry impact is ultimately decided by our ability to attain language fluency, grasp the culture, and establish genuine friendships with people. We could be on a grace-driven, healthy team that loves one another well but is still making no impact on the local community due to poor language/culture development.

◡ꙅ So what can we say about learning the language and culture?

To survive, thrive, and be effective in our mission, we must give top priority to learning the language and culture well before attempting to build any kind of strategy for reaching a people. In addition, we must make sure our home churches, supporters, and agencies recognize this top priority. But the most important person to be on-board with this focus is me! I will need discipline, humility, and perseverance to stay the course and become fluent. Language mastery opens up the culture to us. Cultural understanding gives us insight into the people's worldview. Understanding their worldview assists us in developing a strategy for presenting the gospel correctly and for discerning true seekers and healthy disciples.

Language Goals for the First 3 Years in a Pioneer Field:
1. Avoid using English with locals in the community.
2. Limit Internet, email, social networking time.
3. Arrange for language course and tutors for the whole family.
4. Spend more time with local people than with ex-pats.
5. Establish valid entry points into society to get connected.

John and Kate decided not to get more involved with the international church, at least not until they had mastered the local language better. They renewed their commitment to learn the language well and set out a plan for how they could achieve this goal. John figured out a way to lessen their expenses in order to pay for childcare so Kate could enroll in a language program. While attending the next level in the language program with Kate, John decided to work harder to meet neighbors, visit more shop keepers and even explore ways to obtain part-time work in the community.

Discussion Questions (Group or Mentor)

1. Why is language fluency the top priority in a foreign country?

2. How is it that those seeking to serve cross-culturally could fail to make language and culture learning their top priority?

3. What would you guess would be the greatest hindrances to cultural adaptation and language mastery?

4. What changes have happened in the world in the last 20+ years that actually make it harder to focus on language study and practice?

5. How does language connect with culture? Why is understanding the culture so significant?

6. How do you think newcomers who say they are committed to language learning fall into the trap of spending too much time with ex-pats?

Homework Assignments:

Write out your understanding of the priority of mastering a language and grasping the culture before engaging in ministry. (3-5 pg) Include the following in your paper:

> - Lessons from three missionaries about how learning a language and culture well relates to ministry effectiveness

> - Insights from three missionaries regarding the main reasons why foreigners living overseas could fail to learn a language well

> - Lessons from three foreign believers about the importance of language for a foreigner who wants to minister overseas

> - Your strategy plan to make sure you, your church, and your agency put language learning as the top priority for the first years in country

> - Experiences or achievements you have completed which give evidence of considerable discipline and perseverance

Chapter 13 Notes

1   Paul G. Hiebert and Eloise Hiebert Meneses, *Incarnational Ministry: Planting Churches in Band, Tribal, Peasant, and Urban Societies* (Grand Rapid: Baker Books, 1995), 370.

2   E. Thomas Brewster, *Language Acquisition Made Practical: Field Methods for Language Learners* (Colorado Springs: Lingua House, 1976), 6.

3   Ibid.

4   Andrew F. Walls, *The Missionary Movement in Christian History: Studies in the Transmission of Faith* (Edinburgh: Orbis Books, 1996), 26.

5   "Language Learning Difficulty | About World Languages," http://aboutworldlanguages.com/language-difficulty (Accessed October 17, 2013).

Chapter 14

Working as a Cross-Cultural Servant

What Is Your Attitude Toward The People?

> *"Let him who is the greatest among you*
> *become as the youngest,*
> *and the leader as the servant."*
> *Luke 22:26*

〜' *Tim and Beth arrived on the field over a year ago and were progressing well in language studies. Their language level limited them from being involved in any of the local church plant efforts. They were, however, able to observe and hear about things that were happening within these different gatherings. While there had been several baptisms in the last year and the small fellowships were growing slowly, Tim and Beth had some concerns. It seemed that there were as many people falling away and leaving the groups as there were people joining. The leadership of these house groups were constantly dealing with serious sin issues and conflicts. Some of those who had left were stirring up trouble among the fellowships and appeared to be assisting police forces in applying pressure on local believers. Tim and Beth were wondering if the evangelism methods and church assimilation process were in sync with the local culture and worldview.*

Christian character is required for healthy, successful cross-cultural ministry. Jesus Christ, our ultimate example for incarnational ministry, beautifully exemplifies the character traits needed: *humility, servanthood,* and *perseverance.* Before we pursue our vocation, we must work to see these vital traits formed in our hearts and actions right here where we already serve and live. And others should see them in us!

If we desire to minister cross-culturally, we must enter the host culture with a posture of humility in order to be able to assume the role of a child-like learner and persevere with the nationals until the gospel is incarnated within their local culture. Because foreigners often perceive Westerners as coming from the great empires of the world and already knowing it all, entering as a humble servant is the only way to communicate the message of the gospel correctly.

Entering as a humble servant is the only way to communicate the message of the gospel correctly

In our home countries, we may be respected and honored for our training and experience, but like Christ, we must deny those rights, come as servants, laying aside any superior attitude of leadership. Christian workers who hope to bring lasting change will enter with a mindset that they are arriving visitors. They always remember they are coming as temporary workers to assist the nationals in discovering the best strategy for reaching their own people in a way suitable to that culture.

If we are coming to serve the host people, we will not bring methods and materials from our own cultures, but we will work to leave models and tools that can benefit the local culture best. We want the gospel to be expressed

...coming as temporary workers to assist the nationals in discovering the best strategy for reaching their own people in a way suitable to that culture.

through the local culture and the church to be sustained in a way fitting to the society.

True cross-cultural servants have grasped the power and influence of their own cultures on their worldviews, behavior, ministry approach, and even interpretation of Scripture. Only then can they truly operate with servanthood, unencumbered, and free to embrace the new culture enough to know how to impart the gospel within that particular context. They realize that their own cultural patterns are now useless, and they

actually know less about living in this new place than the local children. They must learn how the gospel should be incarnated into this new culture. As servants they persevere, not expecting quick results in working to renew worldviews that have completely different assumptions about God, man, and sin. As they humbly observe and listen, they learn underlying values and beliefs in that culture (see Illustration above).[1]

Cross-cultural servants desire not to see quick decisions and simple behavior modification but genuine heart conversions and worldview changes through Christ. As many eastern cultures put a high value on being hospitable and pleasing guests, even to the point of ignoring right and wrong, one can question the validity of giving an "altar call" or asking someone if they would like to pray to accept Christ.

Anyone who seeks to declare the gospel across cultures with more than just words will live "*with humility of mind*" and "*regard one another as more important than himself*" (Philippians 2:3). While not denying their own cultural identity, those who want to be effective cross culturally must "*think more of the interests of others*" and the others' culture (Philippians 2:4). Humility is crucial in order to labor diligently to learn the host language well, basically becoming as a child again. Language experts tell us that humbling oneself to learn a language "*is a voluntary act requiring a special kind of maturity.*"[2]

> *True humility enables us to exhibit the rigorous discipline and self-effacement needed to become a learner...*

True humility enables us to exhibit the rigorous discipline and self-effacement needed to become a learner and gain cultural and spiritual insight from locals.[3] God incarnationally entered history, "*enfleshed Himself in our nature so that men could comprehend in the clearest way the meaning of the gospel, and respond to Him."*[4]

Furthermore, Jesus exemplified *servanthood*. Though Jesus could have clung to His own heavenly "culture" and completely dominated people with His personality and power, He *"emptied Himself, taking the form of a bond-servant,"* in order to show the mode of operation in His kingdom (Philippians 2:7). As God, Christ knew everything and could have done anything He wanted by Himself; but instead, He humbled Himself to be helped by others, engaged them in His work, and served them that they might serve others (John 4:6). His servant spirit gave its ultimate demonstration when He *"humbled Himself by becoming obedient to the point of death, even death on a cross"* (Philippians 2:8). He did not come simply to impart principles or set up ministry programs, *"but to serve and to give His life a ransom for many"* (Matthew 20:28). The Cross is not just a truth to be proclaimed; it is as a truth to be appropriated in one's lifestyle. Effective cross-cultural servants take up the Cross and deny their rights. They recognize their ethnocentric attitudes about the way the world should operate and seek to be other-oriented in their actions.

...embrace God's timing in seeing the people reached in a way that is home-grown, reproducible, and effective.

Jesus also exemplified *perseverance*. Cross-cultural servants who seek to be effective in the host culture must persevere to learn a language and culture well. They must persevere as they stumble through the new environment, making mistakes over and over, being "foreigners" day after day. Cross-cultural friendships take time and patience. Christ endured ridicule, and sometimes we do too. Cross-cultural servants must persevere long enough to be able to demonstrate the love of Christ in a way that can be understood by the locals in their language and cultural context. We also need perseverance to embrace God's timing in seeing the people reached in a way that is home-grown, reproducible, and effective. *"For which one of you, when he wants to build a tower, does not first sit down and calculate the cost, to see if he has enough to complete it?"* (Luke 14:28 28).

ꙮ So what can we say about the importance of cross-cultural servanthood in order to be effective?

Every believer needs sound Christian character in any endeavor in life. The core character qualities for effective cross-cultural ministry are *humility, servanthood*, and *perseverance*. These traits enable us to enter with the right posture, learn the language well, discover the underlying worldview, and empower the locals to reach their own people. Christ's own incarnation gives us a clear model for how we should enter a new culture and serve others. Maintaining this kind of humble servanthood is particularly difficult for Westerners, but it is vital for achieving effective, lasting fruit.

ꙮ *After learning from their observations of the present evangelism and discipleship patterns, Tim and Beth re-committed themselves to learning the local language well. They realized that they must humbly listen and grasp the culture and worldview of the people. Tim and Beth had become conscious of what cross-cultural servanthood was about. They were not interested in quick results but sought to persevere at a pace that brought genuine conversions and lasting impact in this new place. Conversations with a few local believers who had known the Lord for some time only confirmed their perspective and plan.*

Discussion Questions (Group or Mentor)

1. Do you believe the people and environment you live in at present welcomes other cultures and fosters cultural sensitivity? Explain.

2. Even though many people from different cultures live in the U.S., why do Americans still remain ignorant of other cultures and worldviews?

3. What do you believe are the main causes for people being ethnocentric, viewing their own culture as the best and correct one?

4. Why are certain Christian virtues essential to enabling us to achieve cross-cultural understanding and impact?

5. Besides a humble spirit, a servant heart, and perseverance, what other virtues do you think are important in this work?

6. What are the best ways to determine if you have these virtues for your cross-cultural ministry?

7. What are ways in which our Western worldview could lead to ineffective evangelism and discipleship in an overseas cross-cultural context?

Homework Assignments

Write out your understanding of the role for cross-cultural servanthood in overseas ministry. (3-5 pg). Include the following in your paper:

> Lessons from three people with cross-cultural ministry experience in the U.S. or abroad regarding the subject of cross-cultural servanthood

> Insights about how these workers were able to empower local believers

> Aspects of the typical Western worldview which differ from Christ's incarnational servanthood approach

> Features of your own background and personality that you believe could hinder your ability to be a good learner and servant in a new culture

> Your plan for training yourself in learning cross-cultural servanthood

Chapter 14 Notes

1 Ralph D. Winter et al., *Perspectives on the World Christian Movement: a Reader* (Pasadena: William Carey Library, 2009), 361-364.

2 E. Thomas Brewster, *Language Acquisition Made Practical: Field Methods for Language Learners.* (Colorado Springs: Lingua House, 1976), 6.

3 Frank Allen, "Why do they leave? Reflections on attrition," *Evangelical Missions Quarterly* 22 (April 1986), 121.

4 Addison P. Soltau, "Missionary attitudes and preparation seen in the light of the history of missions to China," *Covenant Seminary Review* 14, no.1 (Spring 1998), 30.

Chapter 15

Forming Healthy Accountability

Are you walking in the light?

"Be subject to one another in the fear of Christ."
Ephesians 5:21

~ Brian and his family had been serving overseas for the past three years. He met Will at a local Christmas gathering of ex-pats. Brian and Will liked each other and met up one night to go for a walk in the neighborhood. Brian felt comfortable with Will and decided to share with him some of his struggles. Will listened to Brian share about the conflicts he was having with teammates, his wife, and his personal calling. Brian's wife was entering into a period of deep depression, and their marriage was in trouble. Will asked Brian if he had shared these struggles with anyone on his team. Brian said he did not feel close enough with them and was afraid of the implications.

Will felt that Brian had cut himself off and was in a dangerous place for his spiritual and marital life. As Will listened, he realized that in spite of the believers around Brian, he was not living within a healthy accountability network.

The lack of healthy personal accountability stands as a leading cause of personal failure for those ministering overseas. Unless we intentionally choose to establish our own healthy network of personal accountability on the field, we will continue to see workaholic fathers, unhealthy marriages, neglected children, interpersonal conflicts, and moral failures on the field. No matter how well a mission agency policy and team covenant is developed and enforced, lack of accountability can lead to early departure and family breakups. It can also hinder workers from getting good input and exhortation in areas of work ethic, language development, and cross-cultural ministry involvement.

> *The lack of healthy personal accountability stands as a leading cause of personal failure for those ministering overseas.*

As we consider overseas ministry, we must ask ourselves:

- Are we presently living within a network of close relationships that practice mutual submission?

- Are these mentors and peer friendships independent of the normal institutional structures in our lives?

We can maintain good relationships with people at work and even church through casual fellowship, Bible studies, and small talk about news and work, yet still be disconnected from people. We may have plenty of access to accountability but still be alone in our personal struggles at work and home.

In an overseas environment, weekly meetings with a team leader and teammates are designed to create healthy accountability, but this kind of structure does *not* always guarantee responsible living. Genuine accountability happens when I choose to submit myself to others, people with whom I feel a freedom to share my heart and struggles. Accountability only works when I have given permission to these people to ask me hard questions. Unfortunately, these kinds of relationships do not always happen in an institutional structure such as church, an on-field team or agency member-care group. They require voluntary submission.

We must ask on this side of the ocean if we are experiencing healthy accountability relationships which are not based on institutional structures, but on mutual submission to one another. What if, when overseas, we are unable to establish real friendships with those on our team? We could find ourselves in a vulnerable and dangerous position thousands of miles away from home. This lack of communication regarding personal and family problems is one cause of Christian workers' returning home. Whether within one's church or from another church, and whether on a team or outside a team, it is *my* responsibility, not my agency's or my church's, to find people with whom I can walk in the light and be accountable.

> *Genuine accountability happens when I choose to submit myself to others.*

Accountability is *not* and can never be your forcing me to keep the commitments you have put upon me or your making me live out the values that you think I should keep. True accountability consists in my voluntarily asking you to help me keep the commitments that I have already made to God, my wife, my family, my church, my supporters, and my organization. We have made both personal and work commitments, and we will need accountability in both of these areas. We need people who know our deepest struggles, our doubts, and our passions. We must also have people who can challenge our thinking, give us new insight, and sharpen our skills.

As mentioned in chapter 7, a healthy accountability network involves having close friends and mentors both at home and on the field. While having a good support team back home is important, our on-the-field accountability team is vital if we are to thrive and be effective. These people help us develop our ministry skills as well as challenge our personal lives.

ON THE FIELD
A. Ministry Development Team
A few ministry colleagues on the field who can offer mentorship by giving guidance and counsel as we sharpen our skills and mature.
B. Personal Accountability Group
A network of trusted friends on the field (agency or non-agency) to whom we can submit our personal walks and ministries.

Author Robert Clinton in his book *Connecting: The Mentoring Relationships You Need to Succeed* discusses the five key marks of those who finish well in life. Based on his own research, Clinton has found that one of these marks is having a network of healthy accountability throughout life.[1] Clinton has observed that successful leaders have mentors and friends who have known them well and spoken directly into their lives year after year. He suggests there are four directions in this *"circle of accountability"* (*See Chart 2*).[2] He says we need *"upward mentors, those who have gone before and can show the way"*, and *downward mentorees*, those younger people to whom we are constantly giving input.[3] Clinton believes it is helpful to have two kinds of peer mentors.

Internal peers are those with whom we share common beliefs and vocations. These colleagues provide mutual encouragement and keep us on task. *External peers* are those who are outside our common circles and have different beliefs and professions. Missionaries need banker friends, financial advisors need pastor friends, school teachers need home school mom friends. We need both internal and external peers for healthy input.

CHART 2
FOUR DIRECTIONS OF ACCOUNTABILITY

UPWARD
Mentorship
Older, Godlier
Experienced, Wiser

INTERNAL PEER	**The Believer/**	**EXERNAL PEER**
Mentorship	**Leader**	**Mentorship**
Inside Common	**NEEDS**	*Outside Common*
Circles, Vocation		*Circles, Vocation*
Thinking & Beliefs		*Thinking & Beliefs*

DOWNWARD
Mentorship
Younger,
Needing Guidance,
Wisdom & Direction

*Taken from *Connecting: The Mentoring Relationships You Need to Succeed.* Paul D. Stanley and Robert Clinton. (Colorado Springs: Navpress, 1992), 162.

↪ So what can we say about having a healthy accountability system when living overseas?

If we want to be successful in life and ministry, we must maintain a network of people to whom we can open up our lives and work. These mentors can be key sources of encouragement and guidance for developing integrity, discipline, focus, and further sharpening in our lives. No organizational team or member care structure can fully protect us from personal or ministry failures. Whether we are with a mission team or simply doing business as mission overseas, the responsibility lies with us to develop our own accountability network of friends and submit our lives to them. As we consider overseas ministry, learning to walk in the light here at home prepares us for walking this way thousands of miles away.

After listening to Brian for a while, Will shared his deep concerns about the unhealthy place in which Brian and his family were. Brian realized that he had not established a healthy network of mentors and friends in his life on the field. Will encouraged him to contact his home church and seek counsel wherever he could get it. They talked about the options for getting help from the mission agency and other resources. Will committed to assisting Brian in getting the help he needed to arrive at a healthier place of accountability.

Discussion Questions (Group or Mentor)

1. Why would healthy accountability be particularly important in an overseas environment?

2. Why would being on a missionary team not always guarantee healthy accountability?

3. Explain how real accountability is more than meeting with a friend, catching up, and sharing prayer requests.

4. What do you believe is the main cause of people not walking in tight fellowship with each other anywhere in the world?

5. Why is it healthy to have external co-mentors, people who are out of our typical circles of work and faith?

Homework Assignments

Write out your understanding of and experience with walking in a healthy network of mentors and friends. (3-5 pg) Include the following in your paper:

> Lessons from three people who have lived overseas for an extended period regarding

> How they achieved healthy accountability at home and abroad

> Whether this accountability came from their teammates or through other believers in the city or both

> Advice about establishing mentor relationships overseas.

> Your next steps towards developing healthy accountability for yourself and your family here at home

> Your plan for how to secure a healthy network overseas

Chapter 15 Notes

1 Paul D. Stanley and Robert Clinton, *Connecting: The Mentoring Relationships You Need to Succeed* (Colorado Springs: Navpress, 1992), 215.

2 Ibid., 162.

3 Ibid., 167.

Part III Action List
The PLACE

☐ **11. Assess People Group and Church History**
Do your homework on the gospel history, prejudices, cultural barriers, nationalistic attitudes and political climate of your target group by reading up-to-date material and interviewing people there.

☐ **12. Make Plan for Connecting in Society**
Discover how your particular skills and giftings can help you enter the target society with a legitimate identity, get connected to society, and establish close friendships of trust.

☐ **13. Commit to Learning the Language and Culture**
Make sure you, your family, your church, and your agency recognize that language learning and acculturation must be the top priority for the whole family in the early years in the country.

☐ **14. Cultivate a Cross-Cultural Servant Posture**
Humble yourself to accept how different western culture is and how difficult it will be to enter a new culture, listen and learn from locals, and persevere to make an impact and empower the people.

☐ **15. Form Healthy Accountability**
Begin walking within a healthy accountability system here at home with both peers and older people as well as develop a strategy for how to establish and maintain accountability in an overseas environment.

Part III Further Reading

The PLACE

Operation World: The Definitive Prayer Guide to Every Nation. 7th Edition. Downers Grove, IL: IVP Books, 2010.

Foreign to Familiar: a Guide to Understanding Hot- and Cold-climate Cultures. Sarah A. Lanier. Hagerstown, MD: McDougal Pub., 2000.

A Better Way: Make Disciples Wherever Life Happens. Dale Losch. Kansas City, MO: Crossworld, 2012.

Cross-Cultural Servanthood: Serving the World in Christ-like Humility. Duane Elmer. Downers Grove, IL: IVP Books, 2006.

Godly Servants: Discipleship and Spiritual Formation for Missionaries. David Teague. Mission Imprints, 2012.

Ready for Launch

Equipped For Long-Term, Effective Ministry

"...that the man of God may be competent,
equipped for every good work.
2 Timothy 3:17

Regardless of the need or the mission, God desires the right **PERSON**. If we are pursuing ministry abroad, first and foremost, we must ask God and others to search our **hearts** to be sure of why we desire this vocation. Entering a career for which we are not gifted and cannot make an effective contribution, no matter how spiritual or commendable the vocation, is foolish. To find our place to serve, we need to discover our **giftings** and skills. We also need external **confirmation** from others regarding our vocational pursuits. Simply reading this book gives only half the benefit of the material. The real meat of this training is found in working through the discussion questions and homework assignments personally and with mentors. Taking the time to interview those with years of experience in the same line of work is wise and helpful. Those who succeed in the important areas of life surround themselves with honest, wise friends and mentors. These are the ones who can observe our character and giftings. To bring integrity to this calling, we should begin to develop a **cross-cultural lifestyle** now and start engaging with the internationals God has brought among us. We must recognize that we can begin to fulfill our calling right here in our country. Furthermore, in this day and age, obtaining a **marketable expertise** enables us to gain important life skills, support ourselves overseas, create a legitimate identity, and establish a strategic platform in a new society. This job skill can also allow us to live and work overseas for a year, increasing our ability to discern and test our callings.

When we have properly discerned our giftings and callings, we then look for the right **PARTNERS** for our mission. In this new venture, we must make sure our **families** are on board, equipped, and entering the work with their eyes wide open. Developing solid **friendships in our home church** can give us a sound home-base we can lean on as needed. As we consider an extended period overseas, we should understand the role of **mission agencies** and the expectations of all parties involved. Knowing the working environment which will work best for us overseas is key as well. Will we thrive by partnering with a missionary team or by **establishing a platform job** overseas or with a hybrid of both? We choose the partnership and platform which will enable us to thrive in the new culture and make a lasting impact. If we do choose to join a mission organization, it is wise to take the necessary time to get to **know our team** leadership and teammates well before entering this serious partnership. The key to developing a strong team that functions within a culture of trust lies in fostering open communication.

After we have established the right partnerships, we must consider the **PLACE** by **researching the target people** and discovering how we can make the best contribution to the Kingdom there. We will need to figure out what identity we will have as we enter this new culture and how we will get **connected with and belong** in the community. We then must ask ourselves if we are committed to and have the resources for mastering the **language and culture**. After we properly acculturate and gain insight into the people's worldview, we are in a better place to develop a strategy to bring lasting impact for God's Church. If we always maintain the posture of a **cross-cultural servant** who has come to empower the people to reach their own, we have a better chance of success. Servanthood is about Christian character, embodied in Jesus Christ. Finally, in order to remain strong, pure, and achieve long-term effective cross-cultural service, we must set up a **healthy accountability** network of people who can walk with us, sharpen our skills, and keep us focused on the right priorities.

We will achieve nothing without God and His Spirit working within us and going before us in the hearts of the people. By working through the material in this book, however, we have done our part to prepare ourselves for a healthy launch into overseas ministry. We now know ourselves, our partners, and our place of service better.

Let us pray without ceasing, walk humbly before God and man, always treasure our families, and labor as servants to see the gospel flourish among the peoples of the world!

"May the Lamb that was slain
receive the reward of His suffering!"
(Moravian missionaries, 18th c.)

Bibliography

Allen, Frank. "Why Do They Leave? Reflections on Attrition." *Evangelical Missions Quarterly* 22, (April 1986).

"Astronaut Selection and Training." National Aeronautics and Space Administration. http://www.nasa.gov/centers/johnson/pdf/ 606877main_FS-2011-11-057-JSC-astro_trng.pdf (Accessed August 6, 2013).

Augustine. *Confessions.* Translated by Henry Chadwick. Oxford: Oxford University Press, 2008.

Bailey, Richard P. "Who's Turning the Mission Field Upside Down?" *Evangelical Missions Quarterly* 37, (January 2001).

Barnett, Betty J. *Friend Raising: Building a Missionary Support Team That Lasts.* Seattle: YWAM Publishing, 2003.

Borthwick, Paul. *How to Be a World-class Christian: Becoming Part of God's Global Kingdom.* Westmont: Intervarsity Press, 2009.

Bowers, Joyce M., and Robertson McQuilkin. *Raising Resilient MKs: Resources for Caregivers, Parents, and Teachers.* Colorado Springs: Association of Christian Schools International, 1998.

Boyd, David. *You Don't Have to Cross the Ocean to Reach the World: The Power of Local Cross-cultural Ministry.* Grand Rapids: Chosen Books, 2008.

Brennfleck, Kevin. *Live Your Calling: a Practical Guide to Finding and Fulfilling Your Mission in Life.* San Francisco: Jossey-Bass, 2005.

Brewster, E. Thomas. *Language Acquisition Made Practical: Field Methods for Language Learners.* Colorado Springs: Lingua House, 1976.

Calvin, John. *Institutes of the Christian Religion.* Grand Rapids: Eerdmans, 1995.

Cloud, Henry, and John Sims Townsend. *Boundaries: When to Say Yes, When to Say No to Take Control of Your Life.* Grand Rapids: Zondervan, 1992.

"Connected, Yet Divided: Telefónica Survey of the Millennial Generation Reveals Digital Natives Are Optimistic About Their Individual Futures." http://blog.digital.telefonica.com/?press-release=telefonica-millennial-survey-findings (Accessed August 5, 2013).

Corbett, Steve, Brian Fikkert, John Perkins, and David Platt. *When Helping Hurts: How to Alleviate Poverty Without Hurting the Poor . . . and Yourself.* New Edition. Chicago: Moody Publishers, 2014.

Elmer, Duane. *Cross Cultural Connections: Stepping Out and Fitting in Around the World.* Downers Grove: Intervarsity, 2002.

_____. *Cross-cultural Servanthood: Serving the World in Christ-like Humility.* Downers Grove: IVP Books, 2006.

Gordon-Conwell Theological Seminary. "Status of Global Mission." *Global Data Center for the Study of Global Christianity.* www.gordonconwell.edu/resources/ CSGC-Resources.cfm. (Accessed August 6, 2013).

Guinness, Os. *The Call: Finding and Fulfilling the Central Purpose of Your Life.* Nashville: W Publishing Group, 2003.

Hamilton, Don. *Tentmakers Speak: Practical Advice from over 400 Missionary Tentmakers.* Ventura: Regal Books, 1989.

Hay, Rob. *Worth Keeping: Global Perspectives on Best Practice in Missionary Retention.* Pasadena: William Carey Library, 2007.

Hiebert, Paul G., *Anthropological Insights for Missionaries.* Grand Rapids: Baker Book House, 1985.

Hiebert, Paul G., and Eloise Hiebert Meneses. *Incarnational Ministry: Planting Churches in Band, Tribal, Peasant, and Urban Societies.* Grand Rapids: Baker Books, 1995.

Lai, Patrick. *Tentmaking: The Life and Work of Business as Missions.* Downers Grove: Intervarsity Press, 2005.

Lanier, Sarah A. *Foreign to Familiar: a Guide to Understanding Hot- and Cold-climate Cultures.* Hagerstown: McDougal Publishing, 2000.

"Language Learning Difficulty | About World Languages." http://aboutworldlanguages.com/language-difficulty. Accessed October 17, 2013.

Lewis, Jonathan. "Taking Tentmaking Beyond Mutually Exclusive Definitions." World Evangelical Alliance Resources, 2006. www.worldevangelicals.org/ resources/rfiles/res3_56_link_1283199525.pdf. (Accessed August 8, 2013).

Lingenfelter, Sherwood G., and Marvin Keene Mayers. *Ministering Cross-culturally: An Incarnational Model for Personal Relationships*. Grand Rapids: Baker Academic, 2003.

Livermore, David A. *Cultural Intelligence: Improving Your CQ to Engage Our Multicultural World*. Grand Rapids: Baker Academic, 2009.

_____. *Serving with Eyes Wide Open Doing Short-term Missions with Cultural Intelligence*. Grand Rapids: Baker Books, 2013.

Lencioni, Patrick. *The Five Dysfunctions of a Team: a Leadership Fable*. San Francisco: Jossey-Bass, 2002.

Lloyd, John, and John Mitchinson. *If Ignorance Is Bliss, Why Aren't There More Happy People?: Smart Quotes for Dumb Times*. New York: Random House, 2009.

Loss, Myron. *Culture Shock: Dealing With the Stress in Cross-Cultural Living*. 1st edition. Edina: Light and Life Press, 1983.

Lupton, Robert D. *Toxic Charity: How Churches and Charities Hurt Those They Help (and How to Reverse It)*. New York: HarperOne, 2011.

Luther, Martin. *Three Treatises*. Philadelphia: Fortress Press, 1970.

Massey, Joshua. "Hometown Ministry as Pre-field Preparation." *Evangelical Missions Quarterly* 38 (April 2002).

Online Dictionaries. *http://oxforddictionaries.com/definition/english/xenophobia?q=xenophobia http://dictionary.reference.com/browse/xenophobia*. (Accessed on August 8, 2013).

Operation World: The Definitive Prayer Guide to Every Nation (Operation World Set). 07 edition. Downers Grove: IVP Books, 2010.

Patrick, Darrin. *Church Planter: The Man, the Message, the Mission*. Wheaton: Crossway, 2010.

Peterson, Roger P., Gordon D. Aeschliman, Wayne Sneed, and Kim Hurst. *Maximum Impact Short-term Mission: The God-commanded, Repetitive Deployment of Swift, Temporary, Non-professional Missionaries*. Minneapolis: STEM Press, 2003.

Peacock, Michael. *Cultural Change and Your Church: Helping Your Church Thrive in a Diverse Society*. Grand Rapids: Baker Books, 2002.

Quotes About Language. www.quotationsbook.com. (Accessed August 8, 2013).

"Report of the Presidential Commission on the Space Shuttle Challenger Accident." U.S. Government Printing Office, 1986. http://science.ksc. nasa.gov/shuttle/missions/51-l/docs/rogers-commission/table-of-contents.html. (Accessed September 7, 2013).

Remake, Leanne. *Building Credible Multicultural Teams*. Pasadena: William Carey Library, 2000.

Schwartz, Glenn. *When Charity Destroys Dignity: Overcoming Unhealthy Dependency in the Christian Movement: a Compendium*. Lancaster: Author House, 2007.

Sills, Michael David. *The Missionary Call: Find Your Place in God's Plan for the World*. Chicago: Moody Publishers, 2008.

Sittser, Gerald Lawson. *Discovering God's Will: How to Make Every Decision with Peace and Confidence*. Grand Rapids: Zondervan, 2002.

Smith, Gordon T. *Courage & Calling: Embracing Your God-given Potential*. Downers Grove: IVP Books, 2011.

Smothers, David. "Count Zinzendorf and the Moravians." http://www.watchword.org/index2.php?option=com_content&do_pdf=1&id=48. (Accessed September 9, 2013).

Soltau, Addison P. "Missionary Attitudes and Preparation Seen in the Light of the History of Missions to China." *Covenant Seminary Review* 14, no. 1 (Spring 1998).

Stanley, Paul D. and Robert Clinton. *Connecting: The Mentoring Relationships You Need to Succeed*. Colorado Springs: Navpress, 1992.

Steffen, Tom A., and Lois McKinney Douglas. *Encountering Missionary Life and Work: Preparing for Intercultural Ministry*. Grand Rapids: Baker Academic, 2008.

Taylor, William David, and World Evangelical Fellowship. *Too Valuable to Lose: Exploring the Causes and Cures of Missionary Attrition*. Pasadena: William Carey Library, 1997.

Teague, David. *Godly Servants: Discipleship and Spiritual Formation for Missionaries*. Mission Imprints, 2012.

"The Definition of Xenophobia." www.dictionary.com http://dictionary. reference.com/browse/xenophobia. (Accessed September 5, 2013).

Turnbull, H. W., ed. *The Correspondence of Isaac Newton*. Vol. 2 (1676–1687). New York: Cambridge University Press, 1960.

"USA Right Now." *USA Right Now*. http://www.usarightnow. com. (Accessed August 12, 2013).

Van Meter, Jim. "U.S. Report of Findings on Missionary Retention," December 2003. http://www. worldevangelicals.org/resources /view.htm?id=95. (Accessed August 6, 2013).

Volf, Miroslav. *Exclusion and Embrace: a Theological Exploration of Identity, Otherness, and Reconciliation.* Nashville: Abingdon Press, 1996.

Walls, Andrew F. *The Missionary Movement in Christian History: Studies in the Transmission of Faith.* Maryknoll: Orbis Books, 1996.

Whittle, Deseree. "Missionary Attrition: Its Relationship to the Spiritual Dynamics of the Late Twentieth Century." *Caribbean Journal of Evangelical Theology* Vol. 3 (1999).

Wilson, J. Christy. *Today's Tentmakers: Self-support—an Alternative Model for Worldwide Witness.* Eugene: Wipf and Stock Publishers, 2002.

Winter, Ralph D., and Steven C. Hawthorne. *Perspectives on the World Christian Movement: a Reader.* Pasadena: William Carey Library, 2009.